CONTEMPORARY SOUTHWESTERN QUILTS

CONTEMPORARY SOUTHWESTERN QUILTS

MARY EVANGELINE DILLON

CHILTON BOOK COMPANY Radnor, Pennsylvania

Designed by Adrianne Onderdonk Dudden
Manufactured in the United States of America

Library of Congress Cataloging in Publication Data
Dillon, Mary E.
        Contemporary southwestern quilts / Mary Evangeline Dillon.
            p.   cm.
        Bibliography: p. 176
        Includes index.
        ISBN 0–8019–7977-3
        1. Quilting—Southwest, New—Patterns.   I. Title.
TT835.D549   1989
746.9'7'0979—dc20   89-42850
                                                                 CIP

1 2 3 4 5 6 7 8 9 0   8 7 6 5 4 3 2 1 0 9

CONTENTS

CONTENTS

ACKNOWLEDGMENTS

It has taken much time, travel, and research to put this book together. I have been fortunate to have the help and cooperation of many people. I thank all of the quiltmakers who so graciously shared their work for this volume. They are: Ellen Anderson, Ann Arthur, Marva Dalebout, Gail Garber, Helen Giddens, Betty K. Hayden, Virginia Kane, JoAnne Kern, Martha Leeds, Martha Liefeld, Marylynne Lindenfeld, Stan Lucero, Roxanne McElroy, Miles Merkel, Isabel Merrell, Barbara Phillips, Connee Sager, Audrey Spohr, Teri Stewart, and Pat Wilson. By sharing with us their art and their skills, as well as their thoughts about quiltmaking, each has helped make this a special work. An extra thanks is sent to the quiltmakers and their families who welcomed me into their homes and shared so much of their beautiful artwork with me. I feel privileged to count them as friends. I also give thanks and love to family and friends who have been so supportive and encouraged me in my work, especially my mother, a friend and exceptional quiltmaker, who helped with research and in many other ways. This thanks also extends to members of the Tucson Quilters Guild, too numerous to mention, who have been so supportive and encouraging. Finally, I thank the shop owners and guilds who responded to my surveys and spread the word that I was in search of quilts for this collection. Many of the lovely quilts shown here were found through their assistance.

INTRODUCTION

There are many quilting books available today, but few have highlighted the art of the contemporary southwestern quiltmaker. This book is meant to fill that gap by showcasing some of the innovative quilts being made in the region. Ways to incorporate this southwestern look into your own quiltmaking are also shared. The book shows you many styles and designs you can use and also guides you in the steps needed to create your own designs. You will gain an awareness for the design possibilities that exist all around you. I hope the ideas shared here will serve as a catalyst to further creativity in your own quilting.

Today's southwestern quilts reflect a myriad of cultural and design influences. Many have roots in the traditional quilt designs known across the country, but sources for original design also abound in the lives of southwestern quiltmakers. A varied landscape, multiple cultures, and a number of other influences have combined to create a stimulating atmosphere for the contemporary quilt artist.

Dramatic vistas, from sparse rangelands to towering mountains covered with pine forests, offer the quilter endless design possibilities. For example, many a desert monolith has lent its form to interpretation by fiber artists, as can be seen in several quilts presented in this book. Monument Valley, covering an area that crosses the Arizona–Utah border, is a favorite subject of artists using a variety of mediums, and quilters are no exception. Distinctive landmarks and vivid colors provide ample incentive for creativity.

The diverse heritage of the Southwest is reflected in its art. Crafts and designs from the region show elements of many ages, and the designs have evolved as the different cultures interacted with and influenced each other. The colors and precise geometric lines found in the artwork of southwestern Indian tribes have inspired many quilters. The pueblos of northern New Mexico, reminiscent of the shapes found in the surrounding mesas, have also spurred the imagination.

Quiltmaking is as active and varied in the Southwest as it has become in other areas of the country. There are statewide guilds and local quilting groups, as well as shows and festivals, and, as elsewhere, shops specializing in quilts and quilting supplies. Many quilters from the area have told me of their frustration that southwestern quilts and their makers are often overlooked. Unfortunately, in the past there was a misconception that because the area is always hot, quilts are not necessary. Actually, though, there are extremes of climate in the region. Even in the warmer sections there are times when warm bed clothing such as a quilt is necessary. Also, quilts today are enjoyed as much for the art as for warmth. Many of the quilts shown here are displayed as art and were not made for utilitarian purposes.

Both traditional and original concepts have been included in the quilt designs within these pages. The quiltmakers profiled come from diverse backgrounds and offer a number of approaches to their work. In common, they all share a love of quilts, working with their hands, and a special affinity for the great American Southwest.

ONE

TRADITIONAL QUILTS

As in other regions, the story of the southwestern quilt begins with patterns that have been used for years and has a strong foundation in traditional quiltmaking. There are many quilt patterns associated with the area through names that have been given to the blocks. Forty-eight of these blocks are shown in Figures 1-1 through 1-4. Although each block may have several names, only one or two—those most closely associated with the area—are given here. You may know some of the patterns by other names, as these tend to change according to regional influences, events of the time, and other factors.

"Arizona," "Prickly Pear," "Indian Trail," and "Cactus Basket" are names that evoke images of the Southwest. The blocks shown here were chosen for that very reason. It is hard to determine when a block gained a particular name and when that appellation came into popular use. It may be surmised that because many of these patterns have several names and date back a number of years, they did not originate in this area. Many were probably already in use, and the alternate names evolved as settlers began to migrate west. As an example, note that there are several baskets with diamond shaped flowers in the blocks shown (Figure 1-4). This is a relatively common pattern that has many names and variations. The names "Flower Basket" and "Jersey Tulip" gave way to "Rainbow Cactus" in the southwestern region. As another example, one version of the "Dolly Madison's Star" became the "Santa Fe" block.

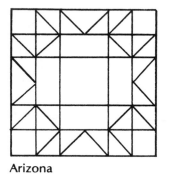

Arizona

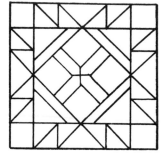

Arizona's Cactus Flower

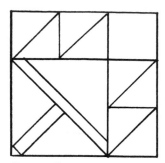

Cactus Flower

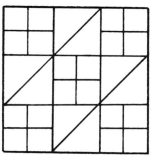

Star of the West
Western Star

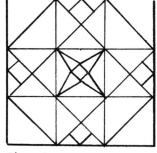

Phoenix

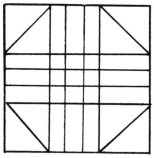

Far West

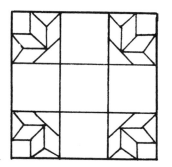

Wagon Tracks

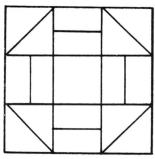

Indian Hammer
Quail's Nest

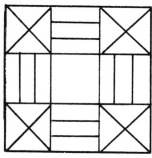

Arrow
Colorado Arrow

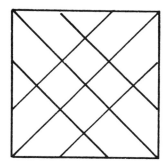

Sage Bud
Mexican Star

The Arrowhead

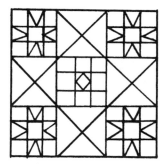

Tangled Arrows

Figure 1–1 Traditional quilt block designs

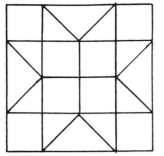

Indian Star

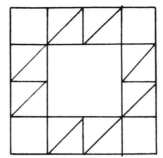

Indian Hatchet

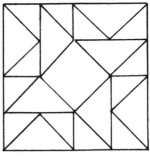

Winged Arrows

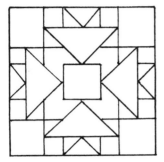

Arrowheads

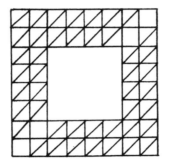

Indian Plumes

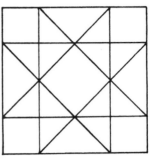

Lone Star
Texas Star

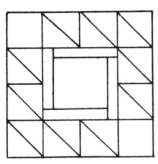

Rocky Mountain Puzzle

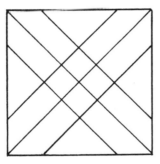

Arrowhead

Arrow Points

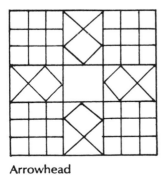

Arrowhead

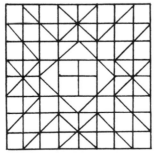

Arrow Crown

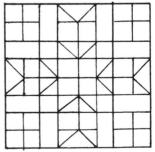

The Arrowhead

Figure 1–2 Traditional quilt block designs

5

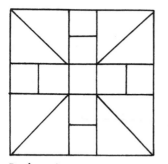 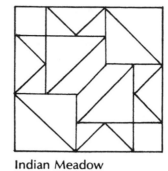 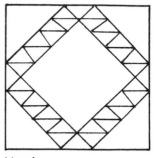

Broken Arrow   Indian Meadow   Navajo
Indian Mats

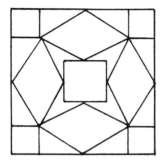 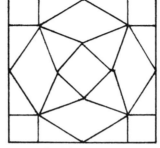 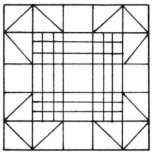

Arrowhead   Arrowhead   The New Mexican Star
Mexican Block

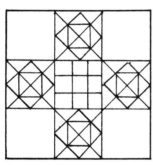 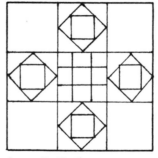 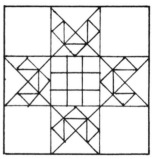

Santa Fe   Santa Fe Trail   Santa Fe

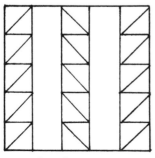 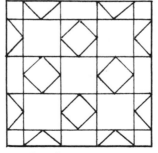 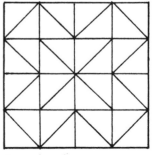

Arrowheads   Devil's Claw   Arrowhead

Figure 1–3 Traditional quilt block designs

6

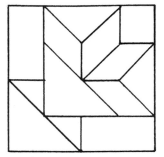

Rainbow Cactus

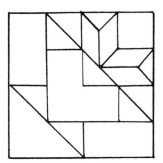

Cactus Basket

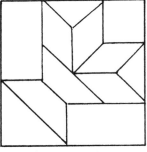

Texas Cactus Basket

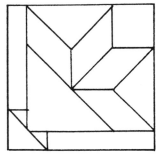

Cactus Basket
Texas Rose

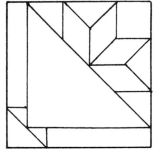

Cactus Basket
Desert Rose

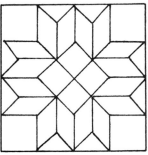

Blossoming Cactus

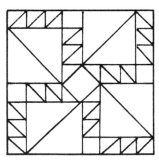

Indian Trail
Prickly Pear

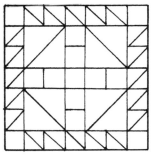

Prickly Pear

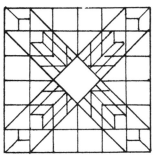

Desert Rose

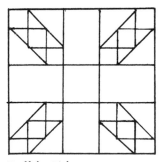

Buffalo Ridge

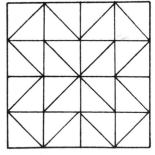

Colorado

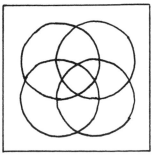

Utah

Figure 1–4 Traditional quilt block designs

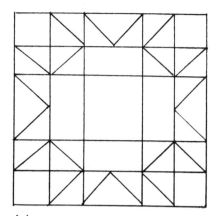

Arizona

Arizona's Cactus Flower

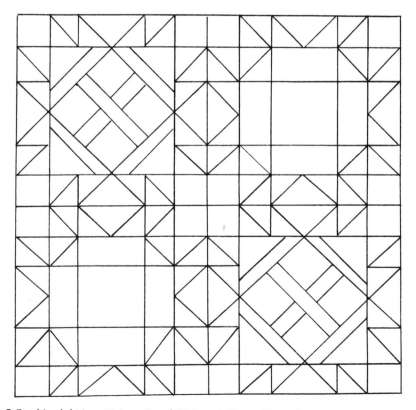

Figure 1–5 Combined design: "Arizona" and "Arizona's Cactus Flower"

This book, showcasing contemporary quiltmakers, is not meant to be a historical record of past works. This brief mention of traditional patterns and quiltmaking is made to acknowledge that as quilters we share a history with others over many years, and that it is only as a result of these ties that our art has been able to evolve.

As in other regions, quiltmaking has been an integral part of women's lives in the Southwest since the 1800s. Quilting has been practiced as a means of providing necessary warmth for families and as an outlet for the creative expression of the maker. A more in-depth study of this history will need to be covered in future works as more research and documentation are completed.

The rest of this chapter examines design ideas for use with the blocks given in the preceding figures. The ideas will help you become aware of all that can be done with the blocks to create quilts with a southwestern look. Even with common designs, each quilter can add a twist, turn, or color that will make that design unique and pleasing in its own way. Seldom will two quilts be the same, which is one of the joys of our evolving art form.

A number of blocks are quite adaptable for use in combination with others. Figure 1-5 provides a good example of how this might work. "Arizona" and "Arizona's Cactus Flower" are very similar in design. The outer row on each block is the same, while the center portions are different. With their similar names and designs, these two blocks are obvious choices to be used together. Each square is created on a 6 × 6 or 36-square grid. As a result, the adjoining lines of the patterns are connected and create an interesting secondary pattern. This pattern can be seen more readily in Figure 1-6.

This technique of combining similar blocks can also be seen in Figure 1-7, which shows a combination of blocks known as "Buffalo Ridge" and "Arrow Points." The adjoining lines are created as the result of two characteristics. First, both blocks are drawn on an 8 × 8 or 64-square grid. Also,

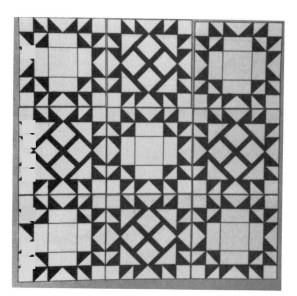

Figure 1–6 The secondary pattern in the combined design of "Arizona" and "Arizona's Cactus Flower" is more apparent in this illustration

each block has a central cross design the width of two spaces in the grid. These two relationships create an ideal situation for combining patterns. Note also that the darker of the arrows is carried from one block into the adjoining block through the use of color, which gives the illusion of one continuous shape. Had a different color or fabric been used in either of the two pieces, the effect would have been altered. Rather than a continuous line flowing

Figure 1–7 Combined design: "Buffalo Ridge" and "Arrow Points"

Figure 1–8 Combined design: ''Indian Star'' and ''Rainbow Cactus''

Figure 1–9 Combined design: ''Blossoming Cactus'' and ''Texas Cactus Basket''

from one block to the other, there might have been an abrupt break in the line. Either way could be considered correct depending on the effect you wish to achieve.

Figure 1-8 shows a combination of the "Indian Star" and "Rainbow Cactus" blocks. A look at the block diagrams shows that both of these blocks are based on a 4 × 4 or 16-square grid. Another characteristic that makes them compatible is that both can be placed on point in a quilt top setting. Using the two blocks in tandem creates a much different effect in the on-point setting than would be achieved with either design alone.

The final illustration of combined designs is Figure 1-9, which places "Blossoming Cactus" and "Texas Cactus Basket" together. There are several characteristics that make this an exciting combination. The most obvious shared property is that of related names. Second, both blocks look best when set on point, and thus are suitable to be placed together. What is perhaps the most interesting result of combining these blocks is that it creates the effect of seeing the basket from two angles. In the cactus basket block, we

Figure 1–10 Four blocks of the "Star of the West" pattern

are looking directly toward the basket. In the blossoming cactus block, proper color placement gives the impression that we are above the basket, looking down into the blossoms as they spread across the top of the basket.

The previous examples are not meant to discount the effects that can be achieved by repeating a single pattern. Certainly the "Star of the West" pattern in Figure 1-10 is an example of an individual block that can be used to create many effects. Lights and darks can be used in this pattern to enhance different areas of the design and thus draw the eye to the area you choose to emphasize. This effect is even more clearly visible in Figures 1-11 and 1-12. These figures both use the "Phoenix" block. In Figure 1-11, triangles in the outer rows and the four-pointed star in the center have been darkened to give the overall effect of an "X" crossing each square. In Figure 1-12 these areas have been finished in a lighter color and the triangles in the middle rows have been darkened. This emphasizes the eight-pointed star within

Figure 1–11 Four blocks of the "Phoenix" pattern, "X" configuration emphasized

Figure 1–12 Four blocks of the "Phoenix" pattern, star configuration emphasized

each block. There are several other options available within this design that quilters might like to try.

The "Broad Arrow" block is another design that allows for several possibilities in piecing. Four blocks of the design are given in each drawing in Figure 1-13. The four blocks are identical, but two results are achieved by rotating the blocks. Figure 1-14 shows the effect if you continue adding and rotating blocks. Figure 1-15 shows how a single block of the design might appear.

Two variations of the "Sage Bud" design are shown in Figures 1-16 and 1-17. Figure 1-16 shows four blocks of the design as it is normally seen. As Figure 1-1 shows, each block has a bud directed outward toward each corner. A second pattern is created when four blocks with buds pointing toward the center are brought together. In this latter configuration (Figure 1-17), the image is reversed, and the block is no longer truly the "Sage Bud" design. To create the effect, the individual blocks were cut apart and then pasted

Figure 1–13 Four blocks of the "Broad Arrow" pattern, in two different groupings

Figure 1–14 Six blocks of the "Broad Arrow" pattern

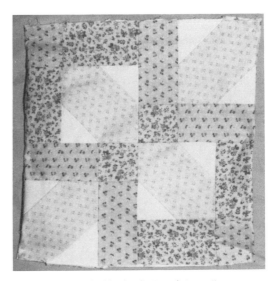

Figure 1–15 Single block of "Broad Arrow" constructed in traditional calicoes

Figure 1–16 Four blocks of the "Sage Bud" pattern

Figure 1–17 Four blocks of the "Sage Bud" pattern "redesigned"

back together with the corner buds pointing inward. With the blocks joined, the buds point away from the center at the meeting of the four corners.

As can be seen from all of these examples, there are an infinite number of ways the designs can be used to create unique but traditional southwestern quilts. You will see as we go along that many of the designs of these blocks reflect the generally accepted ideas of what constitutes southwestern design. I recommend photocopying the blocks several times to try various options. I have done this in many of the illustrations shown here. These duplicate copies can then be cut apart and tried in various combinations. Coloring or painting the duplicates to emphasize different areas will also allow you to explore design options. For many of the illustrations given here, I simply glued the photocopied blocks down on another sheet of paper when I found a combination I liked. Such sheets can be used as a diagram to follow for fabric selection, etc.

An alternative method for experimenting with the designs involves cutting the pieces of the blocks out of several colors of art paper. This works par-

Figure 1–18 ''Winged Arrow'' pattern

ticularly well with patterns that have only one or two pieces with frequent repetitions of these pieces. "Winged Arrow," shown in Figure 1-18, is a good example of this concept. I simply cut triangles from several shades of gray and black paper. I arranged them in several ways before I decided which area to emphasize. In Figure 1-18, the dark dominates; therefore the star stands out, and the secondary design creates a windmill effect behind the star. If the star were in lighter colors and the windmill in darker colors, the windmill would become the dominant design.

This paper-cutting method was also used for the "Cactus Basket" blocks in Figures 1-19 and 1-20. In this case, four blocks were cut and secured to the paper. The individual blocks were then rotated to create a variety of patterns. In one example (Figure 1-19), the flowers point toward the outer corners, and the baskets toward the center. In the other (Figure 1-20), the flowers point toward the center.

Figure 1–19 "Cactus Basket" variation using cut paper to achieve design; flowers point outward

Figure 1–20 "Cactus Basket" variation using cut paper to achieve design; flowers point in to the center

Figure 1–21 "Indian Hammer" or "Quail's Nest"

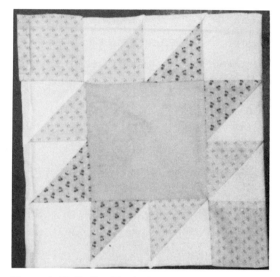

Figure 1–22 "Indian Hatchet"

Figure 1–23 "Indian Star"

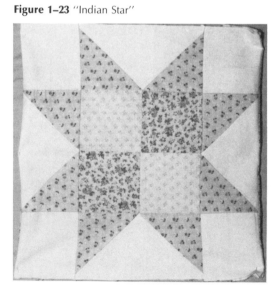

Figure 1–24 "Wagon Tracks"

The remaining illustrations in this chapter give other examples of what can be done with the blocks. Figures 1-21, 1-22, 1-23, and 1-24 are individual blocks, stitched in several fabrics to show the part of the design that is normally emphasized when these designs are made. Notice also that the fabrics in these blocks have a very traditional look—a calico of small floral design with a background fabric of unbleached muslin.

Figures 1-25 and 1-26 show two blocks of a work in progress. These blocks are very much a contrast to the four previous blocks. Quilters are becoming more aware of patterns in fabric design and of the different scales of those patterns. The result is more variety in the types of fabrics available to fiber artists, and they are using these fabrics to their advantage in quilt design. Many fabrics with a "southwestern look" are now available. These

Figure 1–25 "Arizona"

Figure 1–26 "Chisholm Trail"

Figure 1–27 "Arizona Memories" sampler: *clockwise from top,* the patterns are "Cactus Basket," "Arizona" (var.), "Indian Meadow," "Prickly Pear"

contemporary fabrics will give the quilt a modern look even though it has incorporated traditional designs.

Another work in progress is shown in Figures 1-27 and 1-28. This work combines "Cactus Basket," a version of the "Arizona" block, the "Indian Meadow" design, and "Prickly Pear." In addition, the "Cactus Flower" design has been added to each corner. The fabrics were arranged in such a way that the triangles of the cactus flower would be emphasized. This design detail further enhances the southwestern look and feel of the quilt.

The next two figures simply illustrate separate versions of the same block.

Figure 1–28 Close-up view of "Indian Meadow" block

Figure 1–29 Close-up view of ''Prickly Pear''
block

Figure 1–30 ''Prickly Pear'' wall quilt by the
author

Figure 1–31 Typical scene in the Sonoran Desert

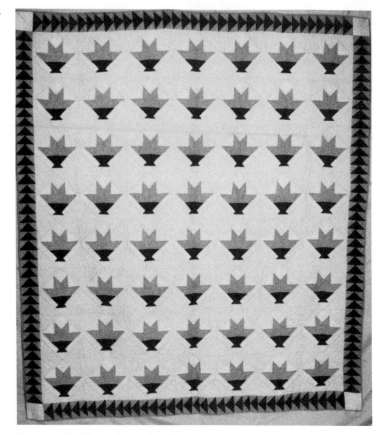

Figure 1–32 "Cactus Basket" quilt by the author

Figure 1–33 Close-up of "Cactus Basket" block

Figure 1–34 Close-up of "Sun over the Mountain" quilting design as used in "Cactus Basket" quilt

Figure 1-29 contains the "Prickly Pear" block from the work in progress just discussed. This is a standard 12″ block set on point. Figure 1-30 shows the same block greatly enlarged to form the center medallion of a wall hanging measuring about 48″ square.

"Cactus Basket" has already been mentioned in this chapter. The block is a favorite traditional design of the Southwest, in part because of the prevalence of this type of plant in the area (see Figure 1-31). The quilt shown in

Figure 1–35 "Sun over the Mountain" quilting design and suggested use for quilt border

Figure 1-32 consists of 56 blocks pieced in brown and green. The plain blocks are of a pale green fabric. A close-up of one block is shown in Figure 1-33. The quilting design for the plain blocks is shown in Figure 1-34. This is a simple design based on the traditional "Moon over the Mountain" motif. Radiating lines have been added to change this to a "Sun over the Mountain" design. The pattern for this motif has been provided in Figure 1-35, along with a suggested use for the motif in a border.

THE QUILTMAKERS

Quiltmakers of the Southwest bring a variety of backgrounds, interests, and artistic impressions to their work. The quiltmakers profiled in these pages took up quiltmaking for different reasons. Many of the quiltmakers I spoke with said they were drawn to create a quilt to express a spiritual feeling about the area. The common thread in their lives is this love of the area and an ability to express this through their work in fiber.

There is a wealth of talent in this region of the country. Quiltmakers included in this volume come from five states of the Southwest: Arizona, New Mexico, Utah, Texas, and California. Although California is usually considered part of the Pacific Coast or Far West region, I have chosen to include the California quiltmakers profiled here because they live in areas of the state that resemble the Southwest, both in landscape and in feeling, more than the coastal areas of the state.

The story of our southwestern quilts is as diverse as the story of any region; perhaps even more so, owing to the many cultures and the influx of people to this area from other regions of the country. This diversity is what has helped make this region one of so many contrasts, and these are expressed in the quilts shown.

Although surrounded by many cultures, the society that dominates in influencing the quiltmakers profiled is that of the Native Americans. Design ideas taken from baskets, pottery, and dances are reflected in the quilts exhibited. These ideas are most often expressed in appliqué, a needlework form that allows the most freedom to express traditional scenes of the area. The majority of the quilts shown use appliqué to express the main idea of the quilt, although a number also include some piecework.

Even with these similarities, the quilters bring their own perspectives to their work. As a group, they have amply captured the essence of the south-western spirit.

ARIZONA

ELLEN P. ANDERSON

Ellen Anderson moved to Arizona last year and within one week had joined a machine appliqué class and started her *Rug Maker* quilt. This project fulfilled two needs for Ellen at the time. First, it provided an outlet to express her impression of Arizona, and she chose to do this in the form of a wall hanging. Perhaps a more important result was that attending the class provided a ready-made group of quilting friends. Ellen was fortunate enough to find a wonderful guild with which she is now involved. Quite a change from the thoughts she had of completing all those unfinished projects while she waited for the opportunity to make new friends and for the furniture to arrive. The free time didn't materialize, and now, like the rest of us, she has many more projects started. There is another interesting twist that made the class and the quilt possible. Ellen may have been without furniture, but she had the all-important sewing machine. Although her chairs and tables had not yet arrived, she found she could sew at her counter. She is definitely a quilter at heart.

Ellen has been quilting since taking a class in Sacramento, California, in 1980. She has produced about twenty quilts for herself and family members. Driving from Colorado through New Mexico and Arizona to her new home in Tempe, Ellen got the idea of making the quilt. *Rug Maker* can be seen in the color section. It is a machine appliquéd and machine quilted piece. Like the other artists profiled here, Ellen has added finishing touches that make the work special. These details can be inspected more closely in Figure 2-1. The first area of interest is the rug that sits behind the weaver. This has been stenciled to give the effect of a woven woolen rug. Next, notice the fine lines of stitching that have been incorporated in the blouse of the weaver. This stitching helps define certain areas of the blouse as can be seen in the collar. It also helps create the illusion of gathers in the blouse as it is bound in by the belt.

This belt is a unique detail that Ellen added to the garment. Making use of small circular silver studs that she acquired at a hobby shop, she attached

Figure 2–1 Close-up of *Rug Maker* by Ellen Anderson

four of these to the fabric. Pressing the studs into the fabric caused the turquoise fabric to push through the small holes in the center of each stud. This created the effect of a silver concho belt with turquoise inlays. A final touch is the care Ellen has taken in creating the hair of the weaver. She wound string on cloth to create a raised effect as if the weaver's hair were drawn back.

The machine quilting pattern for the piece is simple, yet effective. Quilting has been done around each of the mountain forms to accent them. The remaining surface of the quilt is done in horizontal, serpentine lines approximately every two inches. This is a lovely piece, and it is just the first of Ellen's impressions of Arizona.

ANN ARTHUR

Ann Arthur is a quiltmaker from Tucson, Arizona. She has a deep appreciation of and love for many types of Native American art. It is the art of the Tohono O'odham (Papago) basket maker that influenced her to make her *Papago Basket* quilt shown in the color section. Her collection of baskets provided her with the design sources for the nine blocks of the quilt.

The central medallion of the quilt contains a reproduction of the design used on the "Man in the Maze" basket shown in Figure 2-2. This is the Tohono O'odham tribal symbol. The design is found on baskets, in pottery, and in church windows in at least one place on the reservation. This is not unusual as many of the churches have traditional baskets and pottery designs on the walls.

Five blocks of the quilt contain variations of the star pattern, a motif well known to quilt makers. The upper left-hand corner is a representation of the pattern as seen in the basket in Figure 2-3. Directly below this basket on the quilt is a motif that represents what is known as a "negative" basket. This means that more of the devil's claw plant has been used in the weaving and

Figure 2–2 Tohono O'odham basket—"Man in the Maze"

Figure 2–3 Tohono O'odham coiled
basket—five-pointed star design

thus more of the black color is visible. The star appears white and the background black. The opposite, or "positive," of this design can be seen in the middle block of the bottom row. In this motif, the star is black and the background is white. The remaining stars in the middle of the upper row and the middle right side are simplified versions of the first star mentioned. Note that one star contains six rather than five points.

The traditional baskets made by the Tohono O'odham are a form of coiled basket. The most common colors are white, green, black, and a reddish brown. The main coils of the basket are made of bear grass or cattail. A second coil is wrapped around this first coil and stitched to the preceding coil to hold the basket together. The process continues in a counterclockwise progression until the basket is completed. Several other materials are used in making a basket. The white coils are of bleached yucca leaf or willow shoots. The green color also comes from the yucca leaf, but in this case it is unbleached. The reddish brown color is woven of yucca root, and the black areas of the baskets are created with devil's claw.

Ann designed the quilt with the idea of copying the designs found in her collection of baskets, but she also wanted to achieve the coiled look that is such an integral part of the basketry of this culture. She developed a process that combined appliqué and embroidery to achieve this effect.

In the first step of the process, she appliquéd pieces of white fabric, cut to the shapes of the baskets, over batting, stitching these to the red background fabric of each block. Next, by using a pattern of concentric circles of quilting, she gave the appearance of coiling to the appliquéd pieces. These circular quilting lines are visible in the closer view of the upper right-hand corner block shown in Figure 2-4. Also note in this close-up that Ann has imitated one type of rim stitch found on the edges of the baskets. This is known as the lace stitch.

The tedious process of embroidering the designs began after the initial concentric quilting lines were completed. Using the baskets as guides, Ann

Figure 2–4 Close-up of quilting and embroidery lines on *Papago Basket* quilt by Ann Arthur

transferred the motifs stitch by stitch to the surface of the quilt blocks. This was done for each coil entirely around the basket. A close-up of the "Man in the Maze" block in Figure 2-5 clearly illustrates the individual satin stitches on the coils.

Once the embroidery was complete, the blocks were set together. Ann created a dramatic effect in the quilt by adding a black sashing to define both the red and the white spaces of the quilt. She used a quilting design that incorporated several of the geometric elements from the baskets to quilt the center medallion, the inner white border, and the white blocks.

Ann has been quilting for eleven years and has made approximately twenty-five quilts in addition to many baby quilts. The basket quilt is a tribute

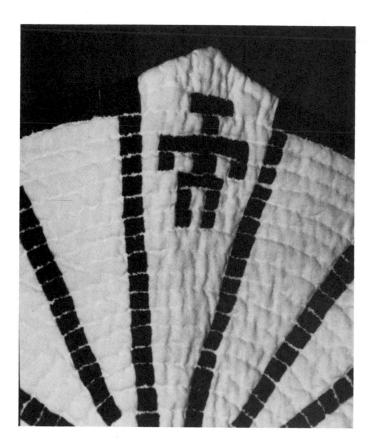

Figure 2–5 Close-up of "Man in the Maze," done in satin stitch on *Papago Basket* quilt

to Ann's skill as a quiltmaker and to her patience in taking the time necessary to produce such an outstanding work.

MARY EVANGELINE DILLON

Two of my quilts have been included in this book. The first is *Southwestern Mother and Child,* shown on the cover. This is my original design wall quilt, and it uses the bias tape method to achieve a stained-glass appearance in fabric. This quilt is one of a series of designs depicting the environment and life of the Southwest that I developed for use in this technique.

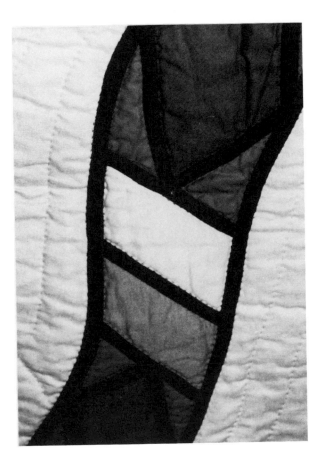

Figure 2–6 Detail of band on garment in *Southwestern Mother and Child*. Note the resemblance to Seminole piecing

To achieve the desired effect in this quilt, I used vivid colors of solid fabrics. The most brilliant colors available were chosen to reflect the vitality of the area. An added effect of these colors is that they all tend to reflect rather than absorb the light. This gives a sense of illumination to the quilt, a desired characteristic in this type of quiltmaking technique.

The piece was hand appliquéd and hand quilted. A line of quilting was placed adjacent to each side of all bias strips, and additional lines were added to give texture to the hair and to create the effect of folds in the garments. A final touch is the use of rays in the background fabric to further give the illusion of light coming from the quilt. A variety of colors of quilting thread were used to match the various fabrics. Figures 2-6 and 2-7 provide closer views of the appliqué and quilting.

An unusual feature of the quilt is the bands of color found on the garments.

Figure 2–7 Detail of appliqué that creates a "leading" effect in stained-glass quiltmaking

I have always admired Seminole patchwork and the way it is used to adorn clothing. I have found through a little experimentation that the effects of this style could be combined with the stained-glass technique.

The other quilt I have chosen to include is *Rainbow Ridge*. It is a simple design and has been included to show that appliqué is not the only technique available to portray southwestern scenes. This small wall quilt was entirely pieced. This is evident in the close-up views shown in Figures 2-8 and 2-9. Figure 2-8 shows the curves and turns that were pieced into the clouds. Figure 2-9 is representative of the sharp angles that can be pieced to achieve the look of the rocky peaks so common in the area.

The number of pieces was kept to a minimum in this work for several reasons. The most important was that I envisioned the picture as being most pleasing to the eye with just a few carefully planned lines, and with unnec-

Figure 2–8 Close-up of *Rainbow Ridge:* cloud, rainbow, and lines in sky were all pieced

Figure 2–9 Detail of piecing and quilting stitch in *Rainbow Ridge*

essary details kept to a minimum. I also wanted to show both the starkness and the beauty of the region. This planning for the design led to two additional benefits.

First, the design was being developed as a pattern for inclusion in my "Blooms of the Desert" pattern line. This meant it would be available to many people with varying skill levels. Next, I wanted it to be suitable for use in workshops for which I have a relatively short time to instruct students unfamiliar with this curved piecing technique.

As with most of my quilts, this piece is heavily quilted. This can be seen in Figure 2-10 as well as the two previous figures. I like the textures and shadings I can achieve through abundant use of the quilting stitch. With the right quilting line, the clouds seem to billow and the striations in the rocks are given depth.

Figure 2–10 Detail of quilting on *Rainbow Ridge*

Like the other quilters profiled here, I have an affinity for the Southwest, and this love of the area is shown in my work. I am a native of Tucson, Arizona, and reside there today. I am one of the lucky ones who first began learning the art of quiltmaking as a small child, and grew up learning all of the needle arts and having a deep appreciation of them.

After finishing college, I became more involved in quiltmaking and have spent the time since then perfecting my craft. This has led to awards on the local, state, and national levels. Now quiltmaking is my full-time career. In addition to writing about the art, I create original designs for my line of patterns, teach in adult education, give workshops and lectures, and research the history of the art form.

BETTY K. HAYDEN

Hours of time and an undetermined number of careful stitches were required to produce the small work by Betty K. Hayden shown in Figure 2-11. This is a prime example of how a finely executed, intricate quilting design will produce a very eye-catching result. Imagine several of these motifs enhancing a quilt top!

The piece reproduces the eight-pointed star design often seen in artwork of the Southwest. She has skillfully combined this with another common southwestern design in the outer quilting pattern. Figure 2-12 gives a detailed view and illustrates how much stitching was actually required to produce the overall effect on the completed piece. Note the rows of stitching placed every $\frac{1}{4}''$ that mimic the coils of the basket. Numerous rows of stitching have been placed between the initial $\frac{1}{4}''$ rows at the appropriate places for the designs to emerge. On average, five to six closely aligned rows were required within each $\frac{1}{4}''$ coil to produce the desired effect. To faithfully reproduce the look of the basket, Betty used a dark thread on unbleached muslin. These colors resemble the bleached yucca leaf and the devil's claw used in basketry.

Figure 2–11 This wall decoration by Betty K. Hayden makes use of common basket designs of the Southwest. Courtesy of the artist

Like others, Betty was inspired to quilt this piece after visiting an exhibit of Indian baskets.

Betty is a native of Tucson, Arizona, and still makes her home there today. She has been involved in the craft of quiltmaking since 1972 and is a prolific quiltmaker. In this time, she has produced eighty-nine quilts. This includes a number of quilts Betty has contributed to charitable organizations in the area. Betty is also active in the Tucson Quilters Guild.

Figure 2–12 Close-up of basket design: note the enormous amount of stitching required to create the effect of a coiled basket

Betty's work is just one example of how a traditional design can be adapted for use in quiltmaking. As with many designs, the inspiration for the original art form came from the environment surrounding the artist. In the case of Tohono O'odham baskets, it was the Sonoran Desert, which spans southern Arizona and parts of Mexico. The giant saguaro cactus is indigenous to this area. Figure 2-13 shows the end of an arm from this sentinel of the desert. Note the pattern formed as the ribs and spines that run the length of the arm converge. Perhaps this design inspired the open-weave basket in Figure 2-14. It is easy to see how an artist examining the work of one medium could see the possibilities for design in her own medium. Quiltmakers have used many variations of this radiating basket design.

Figure 2-15 shows three simplified quilting designs I developed based on observations of baskets. These designs are appropriate in a variety of

Figure 2–13 Arm of saguaro cactus

Figure 2–14 Coiled, open-weave Tohono O'odham basket

Figure 2–15 Three simple quilting designs based on traditional basket motifs

quilts. They can be used on western design quilts rather than the more traditional patterns, such as the feather wreaths, that are often used to quilt large open areas. They are also good alternatives for the quilter with limited time, or for one who does not choose to do the intricate design work as seen in Betty Hayden's piece.

The first motif is the simplest. Beginning with the radiating theme, it simply incorporates the star design that is seen on many baskets. The second motif carries this concept somewhat further. A second row that echoes the first line has been added midway between the center of the circle and the first row of quilting. This doubling of the design adds interest to the motif without greatly increasing the amount of quilting required.

The third alternative in Figure 2-15 adds somewhat more quilting, but it also is more reflective of the radiating effect. This motif was constructed using the same stars shown in the first two examples. In this design, each point of the inner star was divided in half lengthwise, and this line and the remaining half of the point were quilted to form the windmill or flower petal effect. Areas of the design can be made to look more defined by the addition of stippling. This could be done on every petal or every other petal, depending on the effect you wish to achieve.

I also created a motif that incorporates part of what is sometimes called a turtleback design from baskets; Betty created a similar motif which is seen on the outer row of her piece and is shown in Figure 2-16. The motif is divided into four sections, and the resulting cross pattern is also a common sight on baskets. This is a very effective motif to fill large open spaces in a quilt top. Again, the amount of quilting will depend on what effect you wish to achieve. All or parts of the design can be extracted for use. For example, you may choose to do only two or three rows rather than the four that are shown. I have also had pleasing results when I stippled parts of this design and have been able to clearly define various sections of the motif by making use of this technique.

Figure 2–16 This ''cross'' or ''turtleback'' pattern for quilting is common in baskets

The motifs just discussed are less complicated to draft than first appear-
ances may indicate. Circular graph paper or a compass and protractor are
all that is necessary. This technique will be discussed in detail in Chapter 6.
By photocopying and enlarging the designs from this book you can experiment with them and change elements of the motifs as necessary to achieve
the desired quilting design.

JOANNE K. KERN

When JoAnne Kern moved to Arizona, the *Grand Canyon* quilt shown in the color section was designed to celebrate the move. JoAnne's mother, Rose Erickson, also moved to the state, and mother and daughter combined their talents to produce this striking quilt. Rose is a professional artist and JoAnne is the quilter in the family. JoAnne worked from Rose's design to create the quilt. This is the first piece they completed as a team.

In the quilt, birds are seen soaring over the deep gorge of the canyon, while the Colorado River winds below. Gold, rust, and brown fabrics have been used with the more subtle lavenders and blues to re-create the image one sees when looking down upon the canyon from the rim. Trees that stand along areas of the rim have been presented in silhouette to provide added perspective and interest to the composition.

The quilting has been skillfully executed to enhance the design that was begun in the appliqué. The formations of the rocky canyon walls have been defined through careful positioning of the quilting lines. This is readily apparent in the earth-toned formation toward the center of the quilt. The striations that are part of the canyon's character are created on the surface of the quilt through artful use of needle and thread.

The quilt is finished with a border of diagonal strips, forming a V shape in the middle of each side of the quilt. This border is done in the earthy gold, rust, and brown tones of the main body of the quilt and provides a good finish or framing effect for the piece. The careful use of the quilting stitch to enhance what has already been done in the piecing is continued with this border, just as it was in the central design.

JoAnne has been quilting for eight years. She moved to Arizona from the Midwest in 1980. She began quiltmaking while living in Prescott, and she has made approximately a dozen quilts. The masterful piece shown in this collection earned second prize for JoAnne in the mixed-techniques category when it was exhibited by the Arizona Quilters Guild.

MARYLYNNE LINDENFELD

In forty years of quiltmaking, Marylynne Lindenfeld has produced approximately one hundred quilts. Many of these reflect western art and the lifestyle of the area. Three of her quilts are shown in this book.

Marylynne's life on a ranch in Marana, Arizona, is depicted in several of her quilts. She is a member of the Arizona State Cattlewomen's Association, the local Cowbelles Association, and several national groups associated with the industry. Figure 2-17 is a photograph of her *Herd Quitter* wall quilt. This

Figure 2–17 *Herd Quitter,* © 1986 by Marylynne Lindenfeld; hand appliquéd and hand quilted. Courtesy of the artist

Figure 2–18 Detail of *Herd Quitter*

piece brings to life cutting time (similar to a roundup) on the ranch. Wine-colored figures against a beige background create a picture in silhouette. Finely crafted appliqué was the predominant technique used to fashion the piece, but embroidered details were added to complete the scene. Figure 2-18 shows details of the appliqué and embroidery work. Especially notable embroidery includes the tails of the cattle ending in tassels and the barbed wire. Note that the top strip of the wire is broken and curled around as might actually be seen on an enclosure of this type. As is evident in her work, Marylynne knows the subject well and is proud of the area she now calls home.

A more traditional geometric pattern is seen in Marylynne's second quilt, shown in the color section. This is not an original design for Marylynne—several quiltmakers have made quilts such as this one. Marylynne saw the design in a quilt magazine and felt that the bold geometric design worked

Figure 2–19 *Indian Quilt* by Marylynne Lindenfeld. 1980. Hand appliquéd and hand quilted. Courtesy of the artist

to give the piece a southwestern feel. She decided to make the quilt, but also to add to the appealing geometric design with colors that reminded her of the Southwest. This meant strong tones of rust and maroon, plus the blues and grays of the southwestern sky. A variety of solids and prints were used to give texture to the surface of the quilt. She used the string method to construct the quilt and then completed it with a simple pattern of machine quilting.

The striking black-and-white *Indian Quilt* shown in Figure 2-19 was made about eight years ago. While consisting not strictly of southwestern designs, the overall effect is a design that is right at home in a southwestern atmosphere. Five of the nine designs can actually be traced to cultures of this area. The motif in the upper left corner is Marylynne's own design. The center motif in the upper row was inspired by items from a burial mound in Tennessee circa A.D. 1400 which may represent cosmic symbols. The center motif in the middle row is a bear mask design from Indians of the northwest

Figure 2–20 Sun kachina from upper right corner of *Indian Quilt*

coast. A beaded design from the northern woodlands Indians was the inspiration for the motif on the right side of the middle row. The remainder of the designs come from the Arizona–New Mexico area.

The design in the upper right corner comes from a Sun Kachina as represented in the sand paintings of the Hopi Indians of northern Arizona.

Kachinas are the spiritual counterparts to almost everything in the real world. They may represent ancestors, deities, or intermediaries between man and the gods. Hopi men dress to represent these spirits at certain times of the Hopi ceremonial year and it is then that the dances take place. The Sun Kachina does not dance in major performances. It falls into a miscellaneous category and is less significant than many other Kachinas. A close-up of this block is shown in Figure 2-20. It is quite common to see the Sun Kachina depicted this way in Native American art. Note the embroidered design over the kachina's left shoulder. This represents rain falling on a corn plant. This is a frequent subject for many of the ceremonies and the designs of the region. Rain and the necessity for it provide a strong influence in the development of design motifs.

The design in the lower right corner of the quilt comes from a black-on-black pottery piece made by Tonita of the San Ildefonso pueblo of northern New Mexico. This block is shown in detail in Figure 2-21. A combination of intricate appliqué and black-on-white embroidery was used to transfer this design to fabric. Intricate appliqué is not new to Marylynne. She has a special interest in the Hawaiian style of appliqué. She has made several trips to the islands and studied the art while there. Though this quilt was not stitched using that technique, her knowledge of the technique and her appliqué ability are evident in this block.

Figure 2-22 shows the thunderbird as depicted in pottery designs of the Hopi Indians. This block is in the center position of the bottom row of *Indian Quilt*. Here again, finely worked appliqué has been used to execute the design in cloth. Of interest is the white appliqué on the wings of the bird.

Figure 2–21 Detail of San Ildefonso pottery design from lower right corner of *Indian Quilt*

Figure 2–22 Close-up of thunderbird block of *Indian Quilt*

In Hopi art, these white symbols represent clouds. The only embroidery to be found on this block is a single French knot for the eye of the bird.

Next in line on the quilt is the bird design in the lower left corner, shown in close-up on Figure 2-23. This design was drawn by a schoolchild from the Acoma pueblo of northern New Mexico. Again note the delicate appliqué required to achieve the final effect.

At center left of the quilt is a motif from the pottery of the Zuni Indians (Figure 2-24). Marylynne says it is believed that this symbol represents cosmic directions or possibly a cloud-all-alone motif symbolizing the unhappy state of spirit of those who did not take part in rain ceremonies. Both appliqué and embroidery were used to complete this design in fabric.

Marylynne first conceived of the quilt when an elementary schoolteacher brought her a coloring book with designs like those on the quilt and asked

Figure 2–23 Close-up of bird design in lower left corner of *Indian Quilt*

Figure 2–24 Close-up of Zuni pottery motif used in *Indian Quilt*

if Marylynne would make a quilt. Her first thought was "no way" and she laid the book aside for six months. After thinking about it for a while, she decided to experiment with the designs and color. After trying colors she didn't like, and tiring of earth tones, she finally decided black and white was her only choice, and this quilt was the remarkable result.

A very effective design choice was framing each block in a narrow strip of black, then adding white sashing. This sets off each block and maintains the balance of the designs in a much more effective way than would have been achieved with only black sashing positioned between the white blocks.

Marylynne tells an interesting story about her time spent working on this quilt. As she worked, she began to have problems with her eyes and blurred vision, causing the black and the white to run together. With worsening eyesight, she could not see the end of the needle and was quilting by touch.

Figure 1 *Papago Basket* by Ann Arthur, 1980; 82″ × 96″; hand appliquéd and hand quilted; all cotton. Courtesy of the artist

Figure 2 *Amish Desert Sunrise* by Pat Wilson and Pam Thompson, 1987–88; 58″ × 79″; machine pieced, machine and hand quilted; all cotton. Courtesy of the artists

Figure 3 Quilt by Marylynne Lindenfeld, 1987; 36″ × 36″; machine pieced and machine quilted; all cotton. Courtesy of the artist

Figure 4 *Rainmaker*, © 1988 by Stan Lucero; 66″ × 90″; machine pieced, machine appliquéd, and machine quilted; all cotton. Courtesy of the artist

Figure 5 *Rain Bird*, © 1985 by Miles Merkel; 66″ × 86″; machine pieced, hand appliquéd, and hand quilted; all cotton. Courtesy of the artist

Figure 6 *Eagle Kachina,* © 1988 by Gail Garber; 50″ × 50″; machine pieced, hand appliquéd, and hand quilted; all cotton. Courtesy of the artist

Figure 7 *Snake,* © 1988 by Helen Giddens; 70″ × 110″; machine pieced and machine quilted; cottons and blends. Courtesy of the artist

Figure 8 *Balloons over New Mexico,* © 1988 by Roxanne Mc-Elroy; 62″ × 76″; hand appliquéd and hand quilted; all cotton. Courtesy of the artist

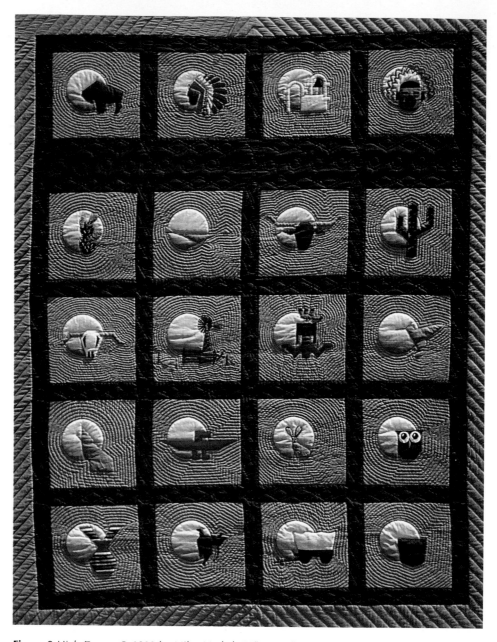

Figure 9 *High Desert*, © 1982 by Miles Merkel; 90″ × 108″;
machine pieced, hand appliquéd, and hand quilted; all cotton.
Courtesy of the artist

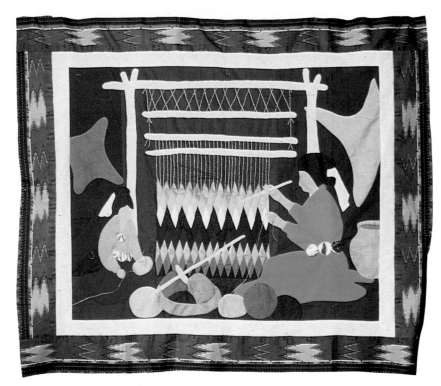

Figure 10 *Navajo Rug Makers,* © 1988 by Marva Dalebout; 60" × 60"; hand pieced, hand appliquéd, and hand quilted; cottons and blends. Courtesy of the artist

Figure 11 *Time for Rest,* © 1988 by Teri Stewart; 30" × 35"; machine pieced, machine appliquéd, and machine quilted; all cotton. Courtesy of the artist

Figure 12 *Deer Dancer Kachina* by Barbara Phillips, 1986–87;
hand and machine pieced, hand appliquéd, and hand quilted;
all cotton. Courtesy of the artist

Figure 13 *Grand Canyon*, © 1985 by JoAnne Kern; 84" × 102";
machine pieced, hand appliquéd, and hand quilted; all cotton.
Courtesy of the artist

Figure 14 *Pueblo Pottery Makers*, © 1987 by Marva Dalebout; 60" × 60"; hand pieced, hand appliquéd, and hand quilted; cottons and blends. Courtesy of the artist

Figure 15 *The Rug Maker*, © 1988 by Ellen Anderson; 25" × 35"; machine appliquéd and machine quilted; all cotton. Courtesy of the artist

Figure 16 *Saguaro Sunset*, © 1988 by Isabel Merrell; 45″ × 54″; hand appliquéd and hand quilted; all cotton. Courtesy of the artist

Figure 17 *Buffalo Women*, © 1987 by Marva Dalebout; 60″ × 60″; hand pieced, hand appliquéd, and hand quilted; cottons and blends. Courtesy of the artist

Figure 18 *Rainbow Ridge,* © 1987 by Mary Evangeline Dillon; 37″ × 42″; hand pieced and hand quilted; all cotton. Courtesy of the artist

Figure 19 *Apache Canyon,* © 1988 by Gail Garber; 22″ × 24″; hand appliquéd and hand quilted; all cotton. Courtesy of the artist

Figure 20 *The Storyteller,* © 1988 by Gail Garber; 33″ × 39″; hand appliquéd, machine
pieced, and hand quilted; all cotton. Courtesy
of the artist

Figure 21 Quilt from *Children of the Southwest*
series, © 1987 by Martha Leeds; 40″ × 60″;
hand appliquéd and hand quilted; all cotton.
Courtesy of the artist

Figure 22 *Armadillo Highway,* © 1987 by Helen Giddens; 72″ × 84″; machine pieced, hand appliquéd, and hand quilted; cotton and blends. Courtesy of the artist

Figure 23 *Coyote and Flowers,* © 1988 by Mary Evangeline Dillon; hand appliquéd and hand quilted blouse; all cotton. Skirt is traditional Navajo broomstick skirt. Courtesy of the artist

Figure 24 *Quail and Babies,* © 1983 by Connee Sager; hand pieced, hand appliquéd, and hand quilted; all cotton. Courtesy of the artist

Figure 25 *Quail and Babies* by Connee Sager. Garment back

Figure 26 *Southern New Mexico Inspirational Quilt* by Sew &
Sew Quilters, Las Cruces, 1982; owned by Martha Liefeld and
Virginia Kane; 75″ × 96″; hand and machine appliquéd, and
hand quilted; cotton and blends. Courtesy of the artists

Being a true quilter, these problems did not stop Marylynne. She installed more lights to try to correct the problem—above, behind, and on both sides. Now, quilting in an Arizona summer can be a warm undertaking, but by this time, Marylynne was getting downright hot. It wasn't long before perspiration caused the thread to stick to her hands. She took to filling the bathtub with water and ice cubes and taking a dip every 20 minutes or so to cool off. She also set her air conditioning unit to 40 degrees. Meanwhile, her husband sat with a sheepskin lined jacket and a quilt around his legs, and decided Marylynne was a very dedicated quilter. This went on for days, but she finished the quilt. Soon after, she had successful surgery on both eyes and saw colors and details she hadn't seen before. She took a close look at her quilt and decided the appliqué and quilting looked pretty good. I'd have to agree with that opinion.

MILES MERKEL

Miles Merkel of Sierra Vista, Arizona, shares two of his quilts with us for this book. The first is *High Desert,* a quilt he designed in 1982. A picture of the full quilt is in the color section.

The quilt is a sampler quilt that depicts stylized southwestern designs of the high desert area. It is constructed of twenty blocks with a tan background set together with a dark brown sashing. This sashing includes a pillow tuck that has been heavily quilted in a geometric pattern. A common point of interest in each block is the strip-pieced sun. This has been appliquéd just off center on each block. Individual designs were then appliquéd and embroidered over the sun to the right of the center. This creates a balance in each design. The close-up of the jackrabbit in Figure 2-25 also provides a good view of the pieced sun as well as showing the intricacy of the embroidery on the quilt.

Miles had decided that some of the intricate areas of the design were not

Figure 2–25 Detail of jackrabbit block from
High Desert

as suited to appliqué work and began to learn embroidery from his wife, Betty, who is an avid quiltmaker. He found he enjoyed the embroidery and could produce the effect he desired in the quilt. As is obvious when you look at the windmill and the fence in Figure 2-26, Miles is very skilled in this area.

The blocks depict a variety of subjects associated with this region. The designs include Indian themes, the missions, the move west, and wildlife, as well as other symbols. Figure 2-27 shows a stylized saddle with embroidery

Figure 2–26 Detail of embroidery and quilting in *High Desert*

Figure 2–27 Stylized saddle design in *High Desert* quilt

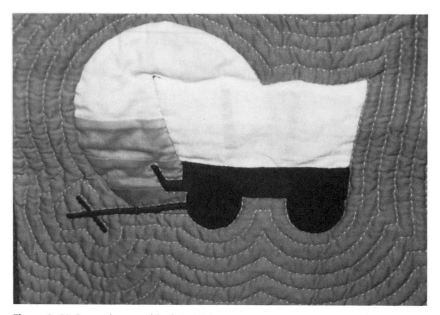

Figure 2–28 Covered wagon block in *High Desert* quilt. Note the shadowing effect of the wood through the cover of the wagon

adornments from the quilt. A finishing touch of special interest is visible in the covered wagon in Figure 2-28. Miles has appliquéd what would be the wooden curved supports that hold the covering of the wagon in place. Over this first appliqué, he has appliquéd the white wagon cover. Notice that the brown shows through the white, creating the same effect that would be seen on a wagon.

Miles has signed his name to the quilt in the block in the lower right-hand corner. The familiar blue denim pocket has the required tag affixed (Figure 2-29), but this designer tag reads "Merkel."

This is a heavily quilted piece. Each block has been quilted in echo quilting in $\frac{1}{4}$" increments, and the lattice has a geometric pattern throughout. Miles considers himself a fabric artist rather than a quilter. He enjoys the designing and the appliqué rather than the actual quilting. But he does realize

Figure 2–29 The "signature block" of the *High Desert* quilt

the importance of the quilting in the overall design. This is always an important part of the process, even though he does not do the stitching. Dorothy Brown of Sierra Vista quilted this piece for Miles, and as can be seen in the close-ups, she is a master of the quilting stitch. The superior workmanship in all phases of construction and many patient hours are evident in this exceptional work, which was awarded second prize at the San Antonio, Texas, Quilt Show.

Miles created *Rain Bird* in 1985. He was inspired to design this quilt after studying a book on Tewa Indian pottery. The black and rust tones frequently seen in pottery have been used against a white background to create an aesthetically appealing quilt. A full picture of the quilt is in the color section.

Twenty motifs have been used in the quilt. These designs were all found on pottery from various time periods. Generally with pottery, the simpler the design, the earlier it was used. Miles experimented when combining the designs to find a balanced arrangement. His first thought was to make use of the motifs in chronological order, but this resulted in too many of the intricate designs falling to one side of the quilt.

Miles has done an outstanding job of both appliqué and embroidery on this quilt. His skill with the needle is very evident. Figure 2-30 shows more closely the sizable amount of embroidery that was required to mimic the fine lines of the pottery and achieve the desired effect. Especially noteworthy

Figure 2–30 Detail of the embroidery, appliqué, and quilting used in the *Rain Bird* quilt

is the precise spacing of the stitching lines and the uniform stitches Miles has used to maintain the integrity of the original design.

An example of Miles's finest appliqué work is shown in Figure 2-31. The checkerboard pattern of the body, the slender legs, and the narrow beak are all stitched precisely. Embroidered detail is also visible here in the oval shapes representing the feathers of the wings.

The crosshatched quilting designs used to finish the piece are visible in both close-up figures. This fine hand quilting was done by Mary Tate. Cross-hatching was an appropriate background to choose for the quilting pattern.

Figure 2–31 Fine appliqué work in the *Rain Bird* quilt

Not only is this type of background quilting popular, but the same type of crossed lines are often seen as a fill-in pattern on pottery pieces. The design has been well used here to accent and bring forth the appliquéd and embroidered motifs, without infringing on these designs.

Miles has been creating quilts for about eight years. In that time, he has designed and made six quilts. His career is as an electromagnetics engineer, a profession that is very demanding of his time and energy. His wife, Betty, is active as a quilting teacher and owns a quilt shop, so when Miles was looking for a form of art to use to relax away from work, fabrics were a natural medium in which to begin working.

Miles's designs are not all southwestern, although he has an affinity for the area and an ability to express this in his quilts. His work as an engineer has led to extensive travel, providing him with varied experiences and impressions to draw from in his design work. This travel has also led to one of his other interests—he holds a black belt in karate. This expert knowledge was gained during a four-year residence in Japan. One of Miles's quilt designs shows this Japanese influence.

Writing is another interest for Miles, and he has two books to his credit. The first is *Smooth in the Saddle,* a novel about the American West published in 1973. His other book, for quiltmakers, is a design book that provides the patterns for the *High Desert* quilt. Miles has published patterns for some of his other designs as well.

BARBARA PHILLIPS

Barbara Phillips is an accomplished quiltmaker from Tucson, Arizona. She has been making quilts for about thirty years. *Deer Dancer Kachina,* shown in the color section, is one of her most eye-catching works.

Her inspiration for this design began when she took a kachina carving class, and after carving her first kachina, decided to put one into a quilt design. During this time, her son requested a quilt with something representing Indian art and showed Barbara a book with an Indian painting he admired. This led to the development of the design for the quilt.

Barbara has taken elements from two paintings and has done a superb job of transferring the essences of the designs into fabric. The paintings were done by two artists of the San Ildefonso pueblo of northern New Mexico. The first painting is *Koshare* by Gilbert Atencio (b. 1930). Koshare is the Keresan name for the figure in the painting, but it was the background of the painting that Barbara used as a basis for the background of her quilt. She then incorporated a figure similar to the *San Ildefonso Deer Dancer* as portrayed in a painting by Tse Ye Mu (b. 1902, also known as Ramando Vigil) into the design in place of the Koshare figure in the original painting. What results is a magnificent piece of quilt art.

To see something painted by an artist's brush so skillfully transferred into fiber is a credit to Barbara's ability as a quiltmaker. A mixed technique incorporating both piecing and appliqué was required to construct the complex design in fabric. Hand piecing, machine piecing, and hand appliqué were all employed in the quilt top. For example, the corn to the left of the deer dancer is appliquéd, and the zigzag line directly below it is machine pieced. Fine black bias has taken the place of the black outlines that were used in the paintings to accent areas of the design.

The accuracy of Barbara's appliqué is especially evident in the flowers on the hem of the dancer's skirt and in the feather-like design in the upper left corner. These have been stitched to perfection. Also observe the beautifully appliquéd circles on the dancer's waist and sash.

Vivid colors and exceptional quilting have completed the transformation of these designs into fabric. The quilting lines have maintained the lines and divisions that were begun in the piecing and appliqué. For example, the appliquéd lightning streak in the upper right corner of the quilt has been echoed by the quilting lines of that area. Vertical lines complement the corn stalk to the left, and give the impression of furrows in a field. In the space behind the dancer, horizontal lines gradually give way to lines that appear to be rays coming from behind the dancer. The quilting lines have helped shape the overall design of the quilt, and the changing patterns of these lines reflect the movements and spirit of the dancer.

Barbara developed this flair for quiltmaking over a number of years and through much experience. She started sewing at a young age, and became involved in 4-H in elementary school. Interest in these activities led her to a major in home economics while in college. She had always wanted to quilt, and after college became involved in the craft. She has produced about thirty-five quilts, many of which display her exceptional appliqué skills, which are so evident in the *Deer Dancer Kachina* quilt.

CONNEE SAGER

Quail and Babies is the charming design Connee Sager has created for her vest shown in the color section. She was inspired to do the design because she loves to watch the quails and their chicks that are frequent visitors to the desert around her home in Tucson. She began by creating a wall hanging, then a vest, and finally what she describes as "oodles of blocks for friends."

Connee was able to find the shape for the quail design in a coloring book that featured desert wildlife of the Southwest. She has taken this basic design and, through skillful use of needle and thread, created a one-of-a-kind piece of wearable art. The garment is hand pieced and appliquéd, hand quilted, and adorned with embroidered details.

Connee has paid careful attention to detail and used some ingenious ways to create the effects necessary to bring the desert scene to life. Connee used cotton fabrics, including bits of cotton lace, throughout the garment. She used several types of lace to create the cactus blossoms. A detailed view of the blossoms on the prickly pear is shown in Figure 2-32. Connee has carefully cut and stitched individual rosettes from lace to achieve this effect.

Figure 2–32 Detail of appliqué and lace
adornment of Connee Sager's vest

Expert appliqué and embroidery techniques were used to create the quails
and the cactus. Embroidery defines the markings of the quail, and note the
especially good use of the embroidery stitch and color to give texture to the
feet of the birds. These details can be seen in the mother and baby shown
in Figure 2-33 and the father quail and babies seen in Figure 2-34. Again,
through a combination of appliqué and embroidery, Connee has been able
to reproduce the distinctive markings of these birds.

Connee's expertise with fabric can also be seen in the color combinations
and prints she chose for the garment. She used the blues and earth tones of
the desert, maintaining a balance between these colors as well as between

Figure 2–33 *Quail and Babies* detail. Note
texture achieved on feet by use of embroidery

Figure 2–34 Detail of *Quail and Babies*

Figure 2–35 *Quail and Babies* wall quilt by Connee Sager, 1988

the light and dark shadings of these colors. All the background fabrics are prints, but these have been varied in type and scale of print to reproduce the texture of the landscape. Flowers, leaves, and fine printed dots are all found on the surface of the garment.

Connee was a speech therapist for many years, but has always worked at one fiber craft or another, including macramé and knitting. She also has a degree in fine arts, so she has always had the desire to be creating something. This need was satisfied by painting until Connee took a quilt class and began to see the possibilities that fabric construction offered. She has been quilting for about ten years, and has made three quilts and numerous wall hangings. She loves to see the final results of her designs in clothing and wall hangings.

Connee has repeated her quail design in a number of pieces. She is especially proud of one small piece completed in the summer of 1988, shown in Figure 2-35. It is a small wall hanging measuring 18 × 22". The quail motif has been appliquéd in the center panel, and the work is completed with a green border quilted with a saguaro and mountain design. Connee made this as a gift for a Japanese quilting teacher, Harumi Tajima, who lives in Tokyo and was visiting Tucson. The motifs are so typical of the Tucson desert that Connee felt it would be the perfect memento for Harumi to take home from her mid-summer visit.

PAT WILSON

Pat Wilson of Gilbert, Arizona, has produced forty-five to fifty full-size quilts and a number of wall quilts in her twelve years of quilting. She began quilting when she discovered a large bag of old quilt squares that had been pieced by her great-grandmother and her great-grandfather a number of years ago. According to family dates, the pieces were about seventy-five years old at the time Pat discovered them. Pat turned these squares into three quilts and seventeen pillows for cousins and other family members so they would have keepsakes from their ancestors. By this time, Pat was fully immersed in the art. She has participated in quilt guilds while living in Iowa, Alaska, and now Arizona.

Pat's quilt shown in the color section of this text is a perfect example of how one can take a completely traditional design and give it a uniquely southwestern feel. She was inspired to make the quilt after seeing an Amish quilt book by Roberta Horton. Pat loves Amish quilts, but also wanted to make a quilt with a southwestern design for a friend. She saw the possibilities of constructing the traditional "Roman Stripes" pattern in colors of the desert. What emerged from this process is the quilt shown, *Amish Desert Sunrise*.

Figure 2–36 Detail of *Amish Desert Sunrise*

The stripes were completed from a number of colors, all of which are vivid colors found in the region. The solid half of each block is a sand color. The quilt is framed by a border cleverly constructed from scraps cut on the diagonal from leftover triangles.

Pat's sister, Pam Thompson, pieced the top following Pat's design. Pat then did the construction and the quilting. An unusual combination of machine and hand quilting has been used to complete the quilt. Hand quilting was used to create the sunrise motif that has been stitched into each sand-colored triangle. This design can be seen more clearly in the photograph in Figure 2-36. Machine quilting has been done in invisible thread along each of the long diagonal lines formed as the blocks were set together on point. These machine lines do not show on the front of the quilt, but still give

Figure 2–37 A sheet with a Southwestern design was used to back *Amish Desert Sunrise*

definition to each block and create a diamond pattern for the back of the quilt.

The southwestern theme has been carried through to the back of the quilt. Pat found a bed sheet that reminded her of the region because of its color and geometric design, and although this type of fabric is not always the easiest to quilt through, she decided it would be a perfect finish for the project. This backing is shown in Figure 2-37.

The quilt was made for a good friend of Pat's in Tucson, and I was fortunate that Pat invited me to be in attendance on the day she was presenting the quilt. Her friend was absolutely thrilled, and the quilt just may be the focal point of an office furnished in southwestern decor. Like most quilters, Pat gives a lot of love with the quilts she presents to family and friends, and for her this is an important part of the art form. She also uses it as her "therapy" and relaxation away from her work as a clinical therapist. It is obvious that Pat loves the art, and she personally takes responsibility for luring at least eight other people into quilting.

CALIFORNIA

AUDREY L. SPOHR

Audrey Spohr of Phelan, California, made her wall hanging, *Roadrunner,* from the original pattern of Pauline Trout. Pauline is a designer from Rialto, California, who has several desert designs to her credit. This quilt, shown in Fig. 2-38, is typical of the desert area of California. Audrey took the original design and added a few of her ideas to create a quilt for her husband, a native Californian who loves the desert.

Pauline's expert sense of design is evident in the composition of the roadrunner. Note the interest that has been added by extending the yucca plants outside the central circle. This desert scene with the mountains in the distance is a typical sight in the high desert of California. When Audrey stitched the design, she added some extra cactus, rocks, and plant life.

Figure 2-38 gives a closer look at the roadrunner. Careful choice of fabric print has created the illusion of a variety of shades of feathers on the bird. Note also that this same technique has been used to create the mottled gray coloring of the rocks. The yuccas are realistically portrayed through good use of the fabrics to create shading and texture.

Audrey chose to use vivid colors in her wall quilt because she sees the desert as always changing and felt strong colors would be more representative of this lively environment. These strong colors at the center are somewhat softened by the lighter green of the outer border of the piece.

Audrey is rightfully proud of the quilting she has put in on this piece. A simple pattern of horizontal and vertical lines at one-inch intervals fills in the blue background of the center panel. The surprise comes in the desert wildlife that Audrey has superimposed over this stitching at the corners of the background. The four animals depicted are a coyote, a quail, a jackrabbit, and a desert tortoise. An example of Audrey's fine work can be seen in the

Figure 2–38 Close-up of *Roadrunner* wall quilt

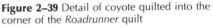

Figure 2–39 Detail of coyote quilted into the corner of the *Roadrunner* quilt

close-up of the coyote in Figure 2-39. In appreciation of this work, Audrey received the Viewer's Choice award for wall hangings when this quilt was exhibited at the 1988 show of the Quilter's Piece Corps of Victor Valley, held in Victorville, California.

Quilting for twelve years, but only seriously for the past two, Audrey has made five full-size quilts, two crib quilts, and the wall hanging. A native of Illinois, Audrey loves her life in the high desert. She says that living there gives her a perfect excuse for quilting at any time. The weather is always changing, and as Audrey says, you can't be outside if it's too windy, too hot, too dry, too wet, too snowy, or too rainy. This leaves lots of indoor quilting time. The only time left is when the earth is quaking, and even Audrey will concede this is not the time to be quilting!

TERI STEWART

In *Time for Rest,* Teri Stewart has produced a piece that will serve as a reminder to her family of the many happy times they have spent on family vacations in the Sequoia National Park in California. A picture of the appliqué and pieced quilt is shown in the color section of this volume.

Teri has combined original and traditional design to create a striking piece of quilt art. The central appliquéd portion of the quilt is Teri's rendition of a Native American woman sitting at a lake in the Sierra Nevada mountains. The woman is Clara Charlie, a member of the Western Mono Indian tribe. Clara lives at the Grant Grove Visitor's Center in the Sequoia National Park, and she is a storyteller. During the summer, the scene Teri has depicted on her quilt is repeated frequently as Clara gives Indian life talks for the visitors to the area. Teri was inspired to design the quilt after camping there for several summers with her sons and hearing Clara speak. The one pattern used in this central motif that was not designed by Teri is the traditional rattlesnake design on the blanket held by Clara.

This central portion of the quilt was completed by machine appliqué, a technique in which Teri is obviously quite adept. Her skill can be seen in the rocky edges of the mountains and in the detail required to portray Clara. A number of pieces were used to capture the lakeside scene.

The borders of the piece were done in black, red, and off-white fabric to create a bold framing of the picture. These colors are frequently seen in the art of the Southwest. The piecework on the borders was also done by machine. Here Teri has used designs typically found in traditional quilts, but these designs are also significant to the woman pictured. The vertical borders of the quilt are taken from an Indian symbol for butterflies. Quilters will recognize the similarity to the often used flying geese pattern. The horizontal borders are made with an Indian symbol for eagles. Machine quilting was used to complete the quilt. This process added texture to the surface of the water by creating the look of waves, as well as giving dimension to the mountains in the background.

Teri lives in Exeter, California, with her husband and two sons. She has been quilting for eight years and in that time has produced ten quilts. Her grandmothers and aunts were quilters as well. Teri was prompted to begin quiltmaking by Ellen Anderson, one of the Arizona quiltmakers discussed earlier in this chapter, who used to live in California. Teri and Ellen are close friends. I had chosen both of their works for this volume and was nearing completion of the work before I became aware that they knew one another. Although neither saw the other's quilt, or even knew of the design while it was being worked, it is apparent that they share a similar style. Both were excited to see how well their quilts complemented each other.

NEW MEXICO

GAIL GARBER

An ability to interpret the spirit of the area in which she lives is evidenced in Gail Garber's work. Home for Gail is near Albuquerque, in Rio Rancho, New Mexico. This area provides ample inspiration for Gail both in the magnificent vistas and in the influence of the Native American culture. She has sewn since she was a teen, and after encouragement from friends, took her first quilt class in 1980. Gail has made many quilts since then, and three of her original pieces are among the works shown in the color section.

Gail has depicted one of her favorite spots in New Mexico in the *Apache Canyon* wall hanging. Figure 2-40 gives a closer view of the traditional New Mexican adobe home that is the central focus of the piece. Especially note two features of the home. Meticulous appliqué of small circles has created the effect of "vigas," which are large wooden beams found in this type of southwestern home. The ends of these beams extend to the outside of the building. The turquoise door is also important to the New Mexican home. It is a long held belief that the turquoise door will keep evil spirits away from the home. The beehive-shaped ovens sitting in front of the home are known as "hornos" and are a common sight in the area. Figure 2-41 shows such an oven that was recently built in Albuquerque.

Notice also the variety of patterns that were used to quilt the mountains behind the home. Gail has done an excellent job of capturing the surfaces found in the canyon areas of the Southwest, and the colors of fabric she has chosen reflect a true southwestern feeling. A special touch in the quilt is the blue fabric for the sky, which was hand painted.

Figure 2–40 Close-up of adobe home in *Apache Canyon* (note vigas—or beams—near top of house)

Figure 2–41 Beehive or "horno" oven

That she should be able to capture this natural scene in fabric is not surprising when you look at Gail's activities outside of quilting. She has a love for the outdoors which is reflected in many of her activities. An avid mountain climber, one of her proudest accomplishments is having climbed Long's Peak in Colorado in 1986. Running also keeps her busy and she has been in a marathon as part of a New Mexico Quilters Association relay team. Designing flower gardens in the Albuquerque area, teaching quiltmaking classes, and developing a line of patterns for her designs are also part of her active schedule.

Eagle Kachina is one of Gail's most eye-catching works. This quilt won first place in the 1988 New Mexico Quilters Association (NMQA) wall quilt competition at the New Mexico State Fair, and it is easy to see that it is a well-deserved prize. In this piece, Gail developed her own design based on a figurine of a traditional eagle kachina and then combined this concept with

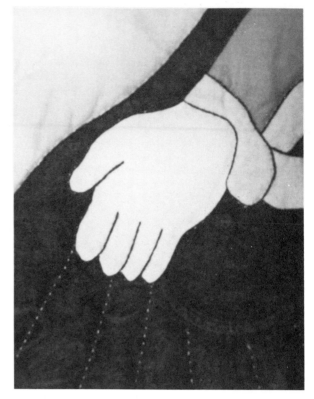

Figure 2–42 Detail of *Eagle Kachina*

a traditional border in the "Delectable Mountains" pattern. Although there are numerous kachinas that might be depicted, Gail says she is fascinated with birds and the freedom that flight allows. Thus she particularly likes the eagle and the owl kachinas. Details of the piece can be seen in Figures 2-42 and 2-43. Note especially the fine appliqué and embroidery work. A black

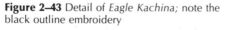

Figure 2–43 Detail of *Eagle Kachina;* note the black outline embroidery

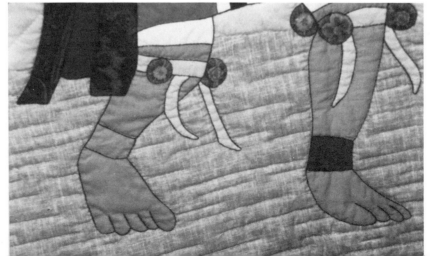

Figure 2–44 Close-up of *Eagle Kachina* showing traditional "Delectable Mountains" border

outline stitch has been embroidered around each appliqué piece to distinguish it from adjoining pieces. This is a technique Gail learned from Fran Soika and one that you will see frequently in her work.

A closer view of the kachina is shown in Figure 2-44. Gail describes her kachina in the following way:

The Hopi Indians believe a kachina is a spiritual being who is impersonated by a man wearing a mask. Kachina ceremonies, or dances, take place during the first half of the year, from winter solstice to mid-July. During the remainder of the year the kachinas reside in the San Francisco Mountains (near Flagstaff, Arizona), the

Figure 2–45 Detail of *The Storyteller;* note the fine appliqué and quilting lines

Figure 2–46 Detail of *The Storyteller*

Figure 2–47 Detail of *The Storyteller;* note the silver buttons on the clothing

Underworld (Hopi heaven), or the Sky. Eagle Kachina sometimes appears at night ceremonies in March. His body is painted black and yellow and he wears wings of eagle feathers on his arms.

The final piece of Gail's is her most recent work and is called *The Storyteller*. This is a delightful wall quilt that captures the spirit of the pottery storyteller figures that are so popular today. The first pottery storyteller is credited to Helen Cordero of Cochiti Pueblo and was made in 1964. Expanding on the "singing mother" figurines depicting a mother and child, she made a pueblo man with five children in honor of her grandfather. These figurines now include representations of people and animals. Gail describes her storyteller in the following manner: "Stories are very important to the pueblo Indians. Often, but not always, the storytellers are grandparents passing down oral tradition, history, and language. Animals, clowns, or mudheads can also be storytellers. The eyes of the storyteller are closed because she is thinking as she weaves her tales to the seven children surrounding her." (Note: not all storytellers are crafted with closed eyes.)

In *The Storyteller*, Gail has again made use of her color sense and her appliqué skills to capture a moment from southwestern life. The closer views afforded in Figures 2-45 and 2-46 show the meticulous care with which each piece is applied, and the fine quilting lines that further enhance the overall design of the quilt. Although Gail does most of her own quilting, Lynn Graves of Albuquerque quilted this piece for Gail. As an added detail, Gail has sewn tiny silver buttons onto the clothing (Figure 2-47). Notice also that a different fabric has been incorporated into each child's clothing to provide even more interest to the design. As in Gail's other quilts, all of this care and follow-through on design have combined to produce exceptional pieces of quilt art.

VIRGINIA KANE AND MARTHA LIEFELD

Virginia Kane and Martha Liefeld are the proud owners of the *Southern New Mexico Inspirational Quilt* created by the Sew & Sew Quilters of Las Cruces,

New Mexico. Pepa Chavez, Francis Dalrymple, Virginia Kane, Martha Lie-feld, Darlene Roberts, Dorothy Roepke, and Betty Speer are the current members of the group. Organized in 1979, they took the name "Sew & Sew Quilters" in 1981. The women are of all ages and come from different backgrounds. The one common aspect of their lives is quilting, and they are happy for this as they believe they would not have met in any other way.

The quilt is shown in the color section, and contains twelve blocks chosen by individuals in the group to represent qualities of life that are important to everyone in the area. All of the designs except for one are originals by the women of the area. Ranching and agriculture are both important in the region, and thus the pecan tree, windmill, and cotton boll blocks were included. "Cotton Bolls" is the only block in the quilt not designed by the women. This pattern came from *Prize Country Quilts* (Oxmoor House, 1979). Technology is important to the area as well, and one block commemorates the landing by the space shuttle *Columbia* at White Sands in 1982. The "zia" symbol of New Mexico has been included in the quilt (top row, center). Hot air ballooning is very popular in the state, and another block celebrates this favorite activity of weekends and fiestas.

The remaining blocks honor the environment and the Spanish and Indian cultures of the area. These designs include an Indian pottery grouping, a thunderbird symbol, and the Church of San Albino at Mesilla, where the Gadsen Purchase was signed. A covered wagon is also included as this was such an important mode of transportation for settlers coming to the area. Martha says there are still a few residents who remember coming to the area in just such a wagon.

Each block in the quilt has special details that make it an individual work of art. Both hand and machine appliqué have been used, and this has been enhanced by generous amounts of embroidery. Figure 2-48 shows a closer view of the superb appliqué and embroidery that was necessary to complete the quilt, in this case showing the pottery block. The colors used in the block reflect the colors of several popular pottery styles of the area.

Figure 2–48 Detail of the pottery design appliquéd on the *Southern New Mexico Inspirational Quilt*

"Spanish Dancers" is the most heavily embroidered of the blocks. This block was designed by Wilma Ziehl, a Las Cruces quilter, but not a member of the group. This pattern was chosen to be included in the *NMQA Collection of Southwestern Designs,* done in 1981. Figure 2-49 shows the extensive embroidery work that was necessary to bring the figures of the dancers to life. Also found in the NMQA book is the roadrunner block. Careful choice of fabric and accurate appliqué combined with embroidery have given character to this roadrunner, which can be seen in Figure 2-50.

Fine workmanship is found throughout this quilt, and the members have

Figure 2–49 Detail of embroidery required for "Spanish Dancers"

Figure 2–50 Detail of block from *Southern New Mexico Inspirational Quilt;* note how fabric used in roadrunner gives the illusion of feathers

done an excellent job of matching their quilting stitches to create a uniform effect over the entire quilt top. Each block contains an individual quilt design that echoes the design of the appliqué or embroidery of the block. In addition, an eagle and mountain motif is quilted in the borders.

The beauty of this quilt has been enjoyed by viewers of several exhibitions. The quilt was shown at and won the Best of Show award in the Southern New Mexico State Fair in 1982. When exhibited at the New Mexico State Fair in 1983, it received second place in the Best of Show judging, and the Gentlemen's Choice award at the Santa Fe Quilt Show. It has also been seen at the Deming, New Mexico, Art Quilt Show, and in 1985 was shown at the American Quilters Society Show in Paducah, Kentucky.

Martha and Virginia are good representatives of the diversity of the group. Martha has been quilting for seven years and has made seven quilts. She grew up in western Pennsylvania, and one of her earliest fond memories is of a "Sunbonnet Sue" quilt on her bed. When she started quilting, she began with that design. Virginia has been quilting for fifty-five years. She grew up in west Texas and remembers carding cotton for the stuffing and helping her mother make quilts when she was a child. She says this was a necessity of life where she was raised, and those early quilts were used to keep warm and not as items of beauty.

The two women purchased the quilt after the group was finished with it, and they currently share ownership. They believe the quilt should stay in the area, but should also be available for the public to enjoy in someplace such as a museum or civic building. It is their hope that one day this can be arranged and that the quilt will find a proper home. In the meantime, they are the guardians of this legacy.

MARTHA LEEDS

An ability to capture the innocence and whimsy of children is what gives character to Martha Leeds's quilts. One of the quilts in her *Children of the*

Southwest series is shown in the color section. This is a series of quilts depicting children of many tribes, shown in typical dress, and against a background reflective of the area in which they live. This series has included crib-size to queen-size quilts.

The quilt shown in this book depicts a boy and a girl from one of the pueblos of New Mexico. The clothes are typical dress. Martha carefully chooses her fabric for the quilts, using fabrics that the garments would actually be made of. Her artistic flair is seen in her color selection and in the combinations of fabrics she uses. Her quilts are all hand appliquéd and hand pieced.

A specialty in Martha's quilts is the extensive embroidered adornment. Notice the gingham shirt worn by the little boy. It is embellished with a strip of embroidery on each side, and his necklace has also been embroidered. In her latest work of an Apache child wearing a beaded necklace, Martha is using intricate embroidery stitches to reproduce the look of the beadwork. Martha's appliqué is as precise as her embroidery. She executes a fine, uniform, closely spaced buttonhole stitch over many of the edges, although others are finished with an invisible stitch. For finishing, the quilts are tied with yarn. The quilts are also evolving as Martha creates newer designs. More recent backgrounds are more detailed and have added points of interest.

Martha has received several awards for her meticulous workmanship. These have included recognition at the New Mexico State Fair, the Eight Northern Indian Market, and at her home Pueblo of Laguna.

The idea for the Southwest children's series was first conceived after Martha saw some dolls of the Southwest and thought that this concept could be transferred into a quilt. She also wanted to create designs that would be enjoyed by children. Martha sees the quilt as a gift the child would delight in having, but also as a means of teaching children their heritage as they observe and learn about the children on the quilt. This concern for children is also exhibited in Martha's other activities. She is very involved with her local school and is running for the school board. She believes strongly in creating every opportunity possible for the students. Her community recently raised the required funds to send the school band to Washington, D.C.

Martha is for the most part a self-taught quiltmaker, although she did learn something about quilting from an aunt. Martha is a member of the Pueblo of Laguna tribe and is also part Pima. She lives with her husband and daughter at Laguna, New Mexico. The area does not have a strong quiltmaking history, although there is some being done at the present. Martha began making quilts in 1980 and since that time has constructed thirty quilts. She sells these quilts at several markets in the area.

A full-time artist, Martha is skilled in a variety of media. She is a painter specializing in watercolor, and one of her activities in this area is painting small watercolors on eggs. She also makes miniature pottery. Adept at cross-stitch, she uses this talent to stitch designs on the kilts worn in ceremonial dances. Martha takes an active part in these dances and fiestas. Beadwork is another interest, and Martha makes use of this skill to create necklaces for the stuffed bears she dresses in authentic dress from several tribes. In addition to all of this, Martha works as a graphic artist and designs logos with a southwestern look for business cards and checks. She seems to come by all of these many talents naturally. Other family members paint and do silver-smithing and beadwork.

STAN LUCERO

Stan Lucero is a neighbor of Martha Leeds in the Pueblo of Laguna, New Mexico. Laguna is one of nineteen pueblos in the state (Figure 2-51). Stan has been quilting for two years and in that time has produced ten quilts. Already sewing, he was inspired to try quilting while watching his wife, Belle Lewis Lucero, at work on a quilt. Stan also has an aunt who quilts.

Rainmaker is the name Stan has given to his quilt shown in the color

Figure 2–51 Church at Laguna, New Mexico

section of this book. This design is the first in a series of rainmakers he has planned. His inspiration for this work came from Native American pottery designs. The large quilt consists of a central motif with the pottery designs set against a turquoise background. Strips of bright color span the length and width of the quilt to frame this central design.

All of the work on this quilt, except for the binding, was done on the sewing machine. Stan is a master of machine stitching, as can be seen in the design found in the center of the quilt pictured. This skill has developed partially through his other work with the machine. Some time back, Stan began making traditional shirts and found that he enjoyed the sewing and that he was adept at stitching. This led him to try some of the strip patchwork as done by the Seminole Indians. He now does quite a lot of the Seminole piecing and incorporates this into the garments he designs.

Stan's designs are very traditional, and yet they are not necessarily assembled in a traditional format. If you examined pottery or other traditional art forms, you would probably not find an exact duplicate of Stan's design. The central motif of this quilt contains elements Stan has drawn from several sources. He likes to select elements from many sources, such as pot shards and petroglyphs, and then combine these individual elements to form a new design. Interchanging these elements does not alter the meaning of the designs. Each element or symbol has its own meaning and could stand on its own away from the complete design.

Stan is much interested in the symbolism involved in the designs. Rain and getting water to the land are a source of great concern for the people of the region. In the art and ceremonial life of the pueblo people, many symbols and rituals revolve around this need for water. In his art, Stan also tends to use symbolism related to this subject. When not working at his own art, Stan spends much time and effort to preserve the symbolism and art of the past for the future. Searching for old pot shards and petroglyphs, he documents any designs he finds. This search covers a large area, so preserving as many of these designs as possible will be a continuing undertaking.

Stan is fascinated by numbers and geometry, certainly a helpful quality when working with the designs he uses. The ability to divide the whole into a variety of sections allows him more freedom when developing motifs to use in his artwork. This ability is apparent in the central motif of the *Rainmaker* quilt. The outer circle of the design is divided into ten equal scallops. The inner section of the motif follows these divisions to a point, but lines and shapes have been added, elongated, and otherwise changed to give several illusions depending on where the eye focuses. One part of the design seems to contain six divisions, while focusing on another area will show four divisions. It takes a skilled craftsman to bring these elements together into a unified whole for a quilt pattern.

Color is another strong area in Stan's quilts. The colors in this quilt harmonize to create a bold color statement. The sharp contrasts between the predominant colors is reminiscent of the Amish use of color in quilts. Aside from creating a striking quilt, he selected the colors for another reason. The turquoise color represents the sky or rain, the brown in the center is mother earth, orange is a harvest color, and the black is for clouds. By using these colors, Stan has maintained the overall theme of the quilt.

As with the other quilters profiled, Stan has many activities outside of quilting. In addition to the quilts and pieced clothing, he is involved in other forms of artistic expression. He does both photography and graphic arts and has created a collection of pen-and-ink drawings for note cards. His drawings reproduce many of the designs found on pottery and are done with meticulous care.

As a tribal member of the Pueblo of Laguna, he has served in tribal government. Stan was instrumental in the formation of Laguna Enterprises, which was developed by the tribe to provide jobs locally for members, and they now work on government contracts. It has been a successful undertaking, growing quite large within just a few years. Stan worked as a manager there until this past year. He decided to leave this job last year to devote full time to his work as an artist. This also allows him more time to spend with his wife and children, and he frequently gives time at the school when extra help is needed.

TEXAS

HELEN GIDDENS

Helen Giddens' quilts begin with basic shapes and some traditional techniques, but from there, an original twist develops in her pieces. Her main interest is in art, and quilting is one of the forms in which she can best express herself. She also does prints and painting, but quilting is taking over as the medium of choice.

Helen created *Armadillo Highway,* in the color section, following her move from Oklahoma to Texas. Armadillos and snakes were prevalent along the highway, and Helen says it could very well be called her ''Road-to-'' quilt. Stylized armadillos in bright red parade across a sand pink background while snakes slither by on their own journey.

Hand appliqué was combined with machine piecing in the construction of the quilt top. Figure 2-52 gives a closer view of the appliqué and piecework required in the design. Intricate piecing was necessary to construct each armadillo. Note how strips of several patterns of red fabric were pieced together to create the illusion of the armor-like bony plates seen on the backs of the animals. As is also apparent, strips of two alternating pieces of fabric were joined together to give the background more texture.

Adding much to the overall design of the quilt is Helen's fabric selection throughout the piece. ''Typical'' calicoes are not to be seen except perhaps for one small white-on-red print used as a strip in the armadillo. Lively checks

Figure 2–52 Detail of *Armadillo Highway*

and large dotted fabrics have been used extensively in the quilt. Especially note the black and white print and how different areas of this print have been emphasized in the various triangles. Helen is obviously adept at using her fabrics in this way to add depth to the pieced and appliqué designs of her quilts.

Helen is proud of the recognition this quilt has received. The quilt received a third place award at the Santa Fe Quilt Festival in 1988. As this text is being written, the biggest honor is still to come for Helen and her quilt. Helen has just learned that the quilt has been accepted for the finals of Quilt National '89.

Helen's most recent piece of work can also be seen in the color section. This work, entitled *Snake,* is a delightful rendition of a creature few of us view as such. The large quilt is an original design that has been machine pieced and machine quilted. Purples and golds are the predominant colors, set against a black and white background. The quilt is an example of superb piecework. A variety of diamond and wedge-shaped pieces of every size were required to create the repeated snake-like rows in the design. This meandering effect is carried through to the border, where the edges of the quilt remain wavy instead of squared off as would typically be seen. Examine this quilt closely, and you will see the rattles of the tail and the long tongue as it darts from the mouth of the snake. The piece was finished with a random machine quilting design.

Helen doodles a lot, and these doodles include snakes and their meandering lines. She was inspired to do this quilt after one particular doodle when she decided she liked what she had done and saw the possibilities for a quilt. She saved this doodle and expanded it into the final design for the snake.

At this time, Helen must fit production of her quilts into a very busy schedule. She is a single parent with three children and a full-time job as a long-distance operator. Although she has been quilting for about sixteen years, when she made the armadillo quilt in 1987, it was her first quilt in about five years. Since then, she has made five others, and she says she doesn't think she can stop! She has made twenty-two quilts altogether. This love of quilts continues a longstanding tradition in Helen's family. Her mother, grandmothers, and great-grandmothers have all been quiltmakers. Helen remembers seeing a "New York Beauty" quilt at age sixteen. She adored the quilt, which was the final inspiration that led her to quiltmaking. Helen plans to continue her quiltmaking, and hopes one day to combine her work in silk-screening and print making with her quilting.

ROXANNE McELROY

Capturing the spirit of a renowned New Mexico event with techniques learned in Tahitian quiltmaking is Roxanne McElroy's unique contribution to this collection of southwestern quilts. Roxanne first became involved in the quilt-making process while living in Tahiti for three years, and this influence is seen clearly in her work.

While living in Tahiti from 1977 to 1980, Roxanne had a housekeeper who taught her to make Tifaifai. This is the Tahitian word for sewing and over the years has come to represent all types of quilts. Roxanne learned to quilt in her present home in El Paso, Texas, in 1986, and at that time realized that all of the Tifaifai she had made were simply quilt tops that had not yet been quilted. She decided to begin quilting some of these tops to make complete quilts. Roxanne then began making more quilts, using both tra-ditional and original designs while preserving the customary techniques of Tifaifai.

Balloons over New Mexico is a sky-blue-on-white quilt with four balloons radiating from the center of the central medallion. The quilt can be seen in the color section. Around the balloons is a zigzag border that reflects the strong influence of Native American designs in New Mexico. Using the traditional Tahitian cut-and-fold method, the central blue motif is cut from one piece of cloth. The fabric is folded into fourths, and all layers are cut at one time, in a process similar to the better-known Hawaiian quilting tech-nique. The design was then stitched to the white background fabric using the needle-tuck appliqué method.

Roxanne is a superb appliqué artist as can be seen in Figure 2-53, which shows the zigzag outer border of the central motif. Note that it was necessary to stitch many exact corners and points to create the overall zigzag or streak-of-lightning effect. Roxanne believes this exactness is possible only with the needle-tuck technique. With other forms of appliqué, the piece can easily become twisted when it is opened because the fabric is folded and many

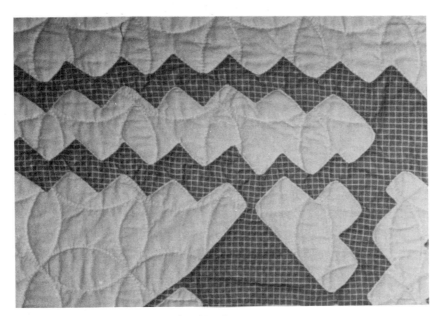

Figure 2–53 Detail of appliqué and quilting in
Balloons over New Mexico

cuts are made. Trying to turn the edge under before basting the entire piece
to the background increases the chance of this twisting. Second, Roxanne
feels there is more control over the amount of fabric turned under, and
therefore points and other small areas of the design can be completed in a
more precise fashion.

Roxanne's quilting stitch is as impressive as her appliqué work. She
achieves thirteen to fourteen stitches per inch, and these are uniform on the
top and bottom of the quilt. She says she was able to achieve this accurate
stitch almost immediately when she began to learn to quilt. Roxanne's theory
is that it is all in her genes. She remembers her grandmother being an exceptional quiltmaker, and her college-age daughter has shown signs of the
same talent.

Besides using a fine quilting stitch, Roxanne's secret to the final look of
her quilts is to include voluminous amounts of quilting. For example, on this

quilt, the words "Balloons over New Mexico" have been achieved as a result of not only quilting the letters, but, more important, doing extensive quilting of the background. This has caused the background to recede and the letters to stand in relief to the surface of the quilt.

As can be seen on the closer view of the quilt, the blue fabric actually has a seersucker look, with a fine white line running through it. Roxanne chose this because it "looked like a balloon." She has made use of this pattern as a guide for quilting the border. Lines of quilting have been done at a diagonal to the lines in the fabric at about $\frac{3}{8}$" intervals, echoing the zigzag pattern of the central motif.

Roxanne now devotes full time to the art of quiltmaking. She teaches the Tifaifai technique in classes and workshops and is always developing new patterns to add to her line of original designs. Some of these designs are derived from traditional old Tahitian motifs, but many are original designs based on Roxanne's impressions of her environment. She has traveled frequently and has lived in a number of places as her husband has been transferred in his work. She has enjoyed each place for the chance to do and see different things. She was especially pleased with Tahiti and now with El Paso because she feels she would not have become involved in an art form she enjoys so much if she hadn't experienced these places. Roxanne's work has been seen at the El Paso Art Festival, the Indiana Quilt Festival, and the International Quilt Festival in Houston.

UTAH

MARVA DALEBOUT

Vibrant colors are one of the first qualities that draws one to Marva Dalebout's work. She has eloquently portrayed the colors and people of the Southwest in what many describe as paintings in fiber. Marva has been quilting for ten years and in that time has made twenty large quilts and forty wall quilts. She took a quilting class, and like many of us, became caught up in the craft in a short time. Three of her wall hangings are included here and can be seen in the color section of this volume.

Navajo Rug Makers is the most recent piece of Marva's work that is shown. It depicts a mother and daughter working at the traditional craft of rug weaving. Marva developed the idea for this quilt while visiting Page, Arizona. She was fascinated by the vivid colors she observed in the clothing of the people, as well as the rugs that were being made. For the most part, the production of the quilt top is carried out in hand appliqué, but there are two notable exceptions. The rug on the loom is hand pieced from a number of diamonds in a variety of colors. The strings of the loom have been hand embroidered to duplicate the look of the warp threads as these are strung on the loom. Notice also the excellent use Marva has made of a printed fabric for the border, which is comprised of a southwestern design and enhances the overall look of the quilt.

The beautiful red rock mountains of southern Utah and Arizona are what first inspired Marva to design Pueblo Pottery Makers. Added to this was a bit of history, imagination, and an admiration of the Native American people. The results of this mixture can be seen in the photograph of the quilt in the color section. Vivid colors reflect the multiple shades of reds and oranges found in the red rock country, and these fabrics have been repeated in the borders of the quilt.

A special feature of this quilt is the reverse appliqué. Figure 2-54 gives a closer look at this. The design of the bands on the robes and the pottery is achieved by carefully executed reverse appliqué with great attention to maintaining consistency in size, as well as accuracy in the individual shapes.

Also note the fine hand quilting and the way the lines of quilting have been used to enhance the design begun in the appliqué. Striations in the

Figure 2–54 Detail of reverse appliqué used
in *Pueblo Pottery Makers*

sky, folds in the robes, and the furrowing of the ground are all visible. The
quilting lines on the white border are composed of triangles and arrows that
create a design with a southwestern look.

Marva has given further dimension to the piece by incorporating darker
fabrics to create a shadowing effect around the figures and the pottery, as
well as giving depth to the openings in the pottery. The care that went into
this quilt was rewarded with a blue ribbon when it was shown at the Festival
of the American West in Logan, Utah, in 1988.

The final work of Marva's that is featured is titled *Buffalo Women*. This wall quilt is also part of her series on Native American working women. The quilt depicts two women making buffalo stew. The plants on the right and left are yucca plants. These plants grow plentifully in the desert of southern Utah and other areas of the Southwest. The blossoms of the plants are worked in stuffed appliqué so that these are in relief to the surface of the quilt. Again on this piece, Marva has used her skills in composition, appliqué, and quilting to create a superb work. Note the shading from gray to light gray to black to create the effect of an open flap on the tent in the foreground, and she has used changes in fabric color and quilting lines to put the mountain range in the background into perspective.

Marva's talents in composition and use of color that are so evident in her quilts come partially from her background as an artist. She resides in St. George, Utah, and is an artist, designer, quilter, and lecturer. She currently teaches quilting at Dixie College in southern Utah. This artistic background leads to an interesting way of preserving the design from each quilt. While many quiltmakers preserve sketches of their designs that they have drawn prior to work on a quilt, Marva takes this process a step further. After each quilt is completed, she paints an exact replica, usually 16 × 20", of the piece in opaque watercolor. This is her way of preserving a record of the quilt.

As has been shown here, Marva is an exceptional quiltmaker. She has won a number of awards for her work, including one of the Top Scorer awards at 1980's Festival of the American West. Another honor has recently been added to this list. She has been accepted as one of the finalists in the Great American Crib Quilt contest called "Childhood Memories."

ISABEL W. MERRELL

Saguaro Sunset properly describes the design of the wall quilt Isabel Merrell has produced by combining a dyed cloth technique and appliqué. The quilt

Figure 2–55 Typical desert scene with storm clouds building

can be seen in the color section of the book. Isabel lives in Brigham City, Utah, but loves the desert area of Arizona and spends part of each year at a second home in Green Valley. She had a desire to put her impressions of the area in a quilt, and this wall hanging was what developed.

Several factors played a part in the final results seen in this quilt. First, Isabel has a special interest in the cloud formations and the magnificent sunsets that are frequent sights in the area. Added to this is an interest in the saguaro and the possibilities this shape presented for appliqué work. Isabel knew she had found the idea for the quilt she wanted to do when she saw a photograph in *Arizona Highways* magazine in 1986. This magazine is well known for superb photographic depictions of the environment and life of the state.

Isabel considered different ways in which the concept might be expressed in a quilt, but the final decision was made after she took a class from Charlotte Anderson at Utah State University. Charlotte suggested that Isabel try tie-dying to create the effect she wanted for the quilt, and thus began the process of transferring the photograph into fiber.

Isabel spent about six weeks experimenting with the technique of tie-dying on various fabrics until she achieved the effect she was looking for. She wanted to be able to show the pink and orange colors of the desert sunset, while also showing the clouds as the dark and light grays play against each other when a storm is building. The photograph in Figure 2-55 gives an idea of the type of scene Isabel was working from to develop her background fabric. Isabel's final choice for this background was an unbleached muslin with a fine white floral print. This was dyed and overdyed in several stages with the black and gray showing through the other colors in some places. Not only has this shown the grayness of the clouds, but Isabel believes that the black showing through the orange and gold creates the appearance of desert shrubbery silhouetted against the sunset.

After completing the background, Isabel began the appliqué process,

Figure 2–56 Silhouette of cactus on *Saguaro Sunset*

Figure 2–57 Detail of stitching on *Saguaro Sunset*

using black and smoky gray solids as her predominant fabrics. The large saguaro in the foreground has weathered many years in the desert, and Isabel interpreted this aging process in the bumps and notches that are readily apparent. She has also added dimension by the sizing and placement of the arms. Figure 2-56 shows the silhouette effect that has been created.

The quilting in this piece begins with a series of random horizontal lines in the sky that are adjusted to the shapes created in the tie-dying process. The quilting lines flow along the lines created by the dye. Lines of stitching have also been used to create sun rays and the furrows of the mountains. An example of these lines can be seen in Figure 2-57.

Although Isabel made what she calls "a few simple quilts" in years past, she says she actually began quilting five years ago after retiring as a kindergarten teacher. In that time, she has taken a number of classes and has made ten full-size quilts and a number of smaller pieces. She has been involved in a variety of needlework activities and had always wanted to learn quilting, as she remembered seeing quilts as a young child. Isabel's love of quilts and children is evident, as is her love of gardening. These affections are intertwined in her life. A large greenhouse at her home in Utah has provided a special project to each kindergarten class over the years. Each spring, the children came from the school to her home to plant a flower for their mothers and a vegetable for their fathers. These were carefully tended until Mother's Day and Father's Day. This has been Isabel's way of sharing her love of the land with the children. She also believes we can instill a love and appreciation for handwork in children at an early age. She sees this in her own grandchildren, who have all received quilts and numerous handcrafted gifts.

Figure 3–1 An assortment of Indian baskets

THREE

NATIVE AMERICAN ART
AS A DESIGN SOURCE

As we saw in the original quilts discussed in Chapter 2, Native American design has had a strong influence on the quilts made in this region. The designs have an aesthetic appeal to a wide range of people and therefore have become a popular design source.

The diversity found in the art seems to provide a never-ending source of ideas to the fiber artist. These designs are often inspired by ancient cultures, but can also be expressed superbly in contemporary form. The motifs are as varied as the environments and cultures in which they began. The designs range from the bold to the subtle, from the simplicity of some geometric designs to the complexity of others, from stylized to highly realistic, and from plain to ornate. The designs are popular also because they are adaptable to so many decorating styles. Some of the geometric patterns especially may be as comfortable in a Victorian parlor as in a room with modern, Santa Fe–style furniture. This chapter will show a few additional examples of how southwestern designs can be adapted for use in quiltmaking.

Figure 3-1 shows a small grouping of Indian baskets, a favorite source of design. Take a closer look at some of the baskets, and you will begin to see innumerable design possibilities. For example, note that a star-like or blossom design is used on several baskets. Numbers of petals in the design may vary greatly. This leaves open the possibility for creating any number of appliqué or quilting motifs depending on your preference. If you see elements you like from one basket, pull these out and combine them with elements of another design to create a new pattern.

The feather design is a favorite element in pottery and basket designs, as well as in jewelry and other crafts. This design also takes many shapes and forms. Some of these are shown in Figures 3-2 and 3-3. Note that the number and width of the feathers may change. The center of the circle can be decreased or enlarged depending on the desired effect. Although not shown in these examples, you might also decide to alternate narrow and

Figure 3–2 Two variations of the feather design common in many southwestern art forms

Figure 3–3 Note how the size of the central circle can be varied to alter the look of the design in these further variations of the feather design

wide feathers or the direction in which the feathers are pointing. I suggest you trace the designs onto tracing paper. You can then lay one motif over another to try several possibilities.

Positive and negative effects of the same design are common in Native American art. For example, the five-pointed star motif woven into the baskets shown in Figures 3-4 and 3-5 is the same design, although there is a slight variation in the width of the points of the tips of the star. However, in one

Figure 3–4 Five-pointed star motif shown in "positive" basket

Figure 3–5 Five-pointed star motif shown in "negative" basket

basket the star is black and the background is white. In the second basket, the colors have been reversed; the star is white and the background is black. The second basket is thus the "negative" of the first design.

Making use of this positive–negative effect may result in some interesting combinations for the fiber artist in developing patterns. In the design presented, the black star appears to be imposed on the white basket. This design would work readily in appliqué. Or the white star could be appliquéd on a black fabric. But a more interesting result can be achieved by stitching black onto white in the second basket to create a reverse appliqué block. A combination of the two techniques might also be used to create the effect of a star within a star when the positive and negative are combined.

Pottery also provides a rich source of design inspiration for the quiltmaker, as we saw in Chapter 2. Stars, diamonds, triangles, and straight and curvilinear designs are common in much of southwestern pottery. Many of the designs presented in this book originate in pottery. Not all of the designs are immediately clear or need to be taken directly as they appear on the pottery. When developing an idea for a design, look at the piece from every angle to obtain different perspectives on design.

Figure 3-6 shows an example of this concept. It is a relatively simple design taken from pottery and adapted to a quilt design, but the figure was not seen in this form on the side of a pottery vessel as you might expect. Look closely at the top design, and the large center circle may begin to appear to be an opening. Indeed, this design was obtained by looking down at a piece of pottery from directly above. The sides of this particular piece flared out, and the design given is how a portion of the pottery design appeared from above as it encircled the vessel. In the lower part of the figure, you will see how the motif would appear if it were straightened to form a pattern that might be used in a border to accompany the original motif.

In addition to being suitable for a single-line quilting design, this motif might also be used for appliqué and reverse appliqué. It is a design that is common on black-on-black pottery, and this effect might be achieved by using gray and black fabric in appliqué. Rust and black would also be a striking combination, although it would certainly not be necessary to work only in traditional colors.

Various forms of scrolling are frequently seen on pottery. The scroll might be an individual element or a repetitive pattern. A variety of rope and scroll-like designs have been used for quilted borders as this style is suitable for needlework. Many of these scroll designs taken from pottery could be readily adapted to quilt styles other than those with a southwestern design.

One such scroll design is seen in Figure 3-7. This is an adaptation of a design found on a piece of Tohono O'odham pottery. It can best be described as an interlocking scroll. This particular design is highly adaptive to quilting as the distance between individual elements of the design can be adjusted to fit the length of borders. The gently curving shape will also complement a number of quilt patterns and might be considered for use in areas where

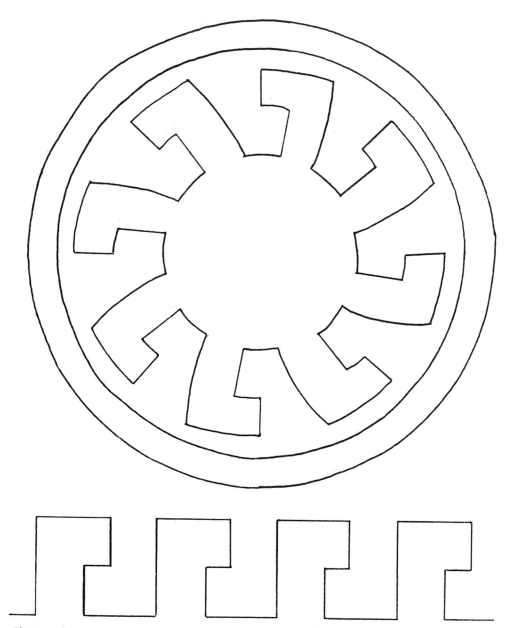

Figure 3–6 Pottery design adapted to quilting motif for block and border

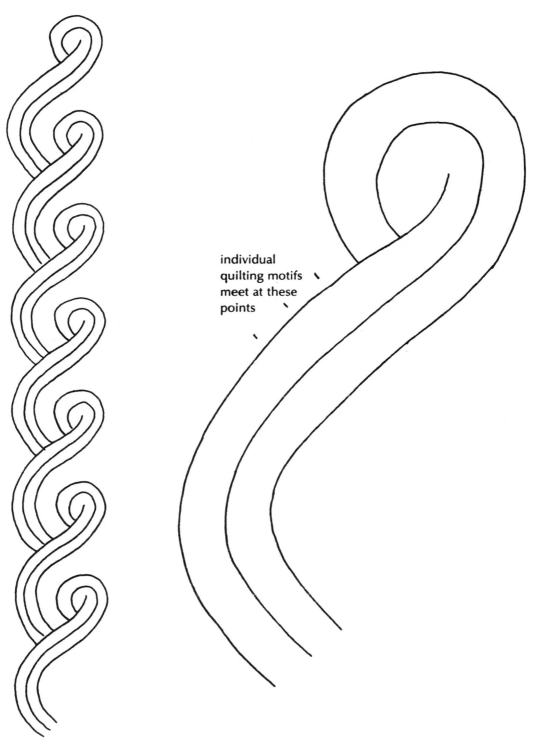

individual
quilting motifs
meet at these
points

Figure 3–7 Interlocking scroll design typical of pottery and adapted for a quilted border

Figure 3–8 This small rug is typical of southwestern weaving

one might otherwise place a feather or cable border. An individual element of the border has also been given to show how the template should appear and where the joining of individual elements would occur.

Weaving is another popular art form in the region, and the geometric designs found in weaving are often adapted for use in other art forms. Figure

3-8 shows a typical rug of the area with a relatively plain design. Although such woven rugs often have more complex and intricate designs, this rug is an excellent example of how one design element can be drawn from an object and altered to create patterns suitable for patchwork, appliqué, or quilting.

As Figure 3-8 shows, the design is built up in a step-like manner with the length of the lines increasing on each step until the center line is reached. The lines are then decreased to form the reverse image of the first half. The motif in Figure 3-9 (top) was developed using this technique. This figure has only two steps, but more might be added to increase the width. The figure shown might be used as a quilting design for a border. Or the strips could be cut from fabric and pieced together and this unit used for appliqué. A third option is to use the pattern as a pieced border. The bottom part of Figure 3-9 shows how elements can be added to "square off" the design, thus creating a rectangular unit. The unit is then repeated to form a pieced

Figure 3–9 Quilt designs based on a weaving pattern

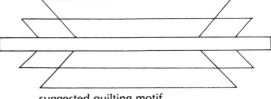

suggested quilting motif

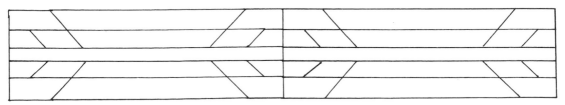

rectangular units that can be pieced

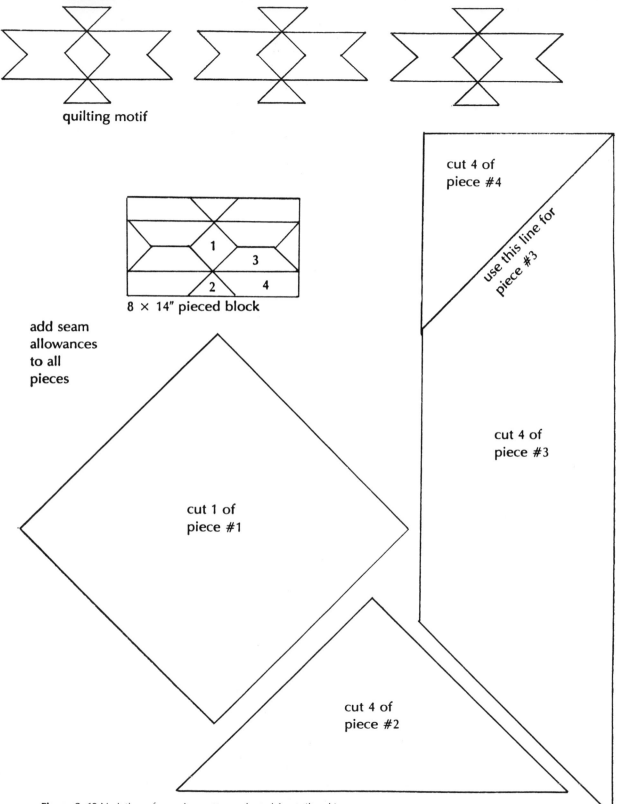

quilting motif

cut 4 of
piece #4

use this line for
piece #3

1
3
2
4

8 × 14" pieced block

add seam
allowances
to all
pieces

cut 4 of
piece #3

cut 1 of
piece #1

cut 4 of
piece #2

Figure 3–10 Variation of weaving pattern adapted for quiltmaking

Figure 3–11 Four border motifs, all developed from a single basic element—the triangle

border pattern. Note also that a secondary design is created when the sections are joined together. This secondary design can be either highlighted or subdued depending on color selection.

The motif shown in Figure 3-10 is another variation of this same design. This, too, could be used for quilting or piecework. In this case, the design contains two rows for each half, and a diamond has been set in the center to provide a focal point. Diamonds are also formed when the individual units are joined. Patterns have been provided with this design to make the square as shown. The patterns given will make an 8 × 14″ block.

Figure 3-11 provides an exercise in how a design might be developed. I created the top border pattern by sketching a motif that is seen frequently in a number of regional art forms. This initial design consists simply of two horizontal triangles and two smaller vertical triangles arranged in a cross-like pattern. This motif can be repeated to complete the length of the area to be quilted. Note that the design is quite flexible. The triangles can be spaced farther apart or brought closer to shorten or lengthen the motif to fit any number of areas. The distance between individual motifs can also be varied to fit a defined space.

The three border patterns that follow this initial concept were all built on the first border. The second border shown is the simplest variation. Here, two close rows of quilting have been added to each side of the row of triangles. The third design illustrates how one small change can make a noticeable difference in the design that will develop. Only one small triangle has been added to each of the side triangles, but this simple addition is sufficient to create a more engaging design.

The addition of another element to the motif will create an even more sophisticated design. In the final border shown, a line of quilting was added to the outside of each of the upper and lower triangles. The line was stopped before it reached the point where it would form a triangle. The small triangle added in the third border was also maintained. The result is that a more decorative border has developed through the addition of only a few simple quilting lines.

I suggest you start with the basic border given and try variations of your own that you find pleasing. An easy way to accomplish this is to place tracing paper over the initial border and try adding or subtracting lines. This way you can try a multitude of variations without having to draw the initial design

Figure 3–12 Navajo rug design adapted for quiltmaking

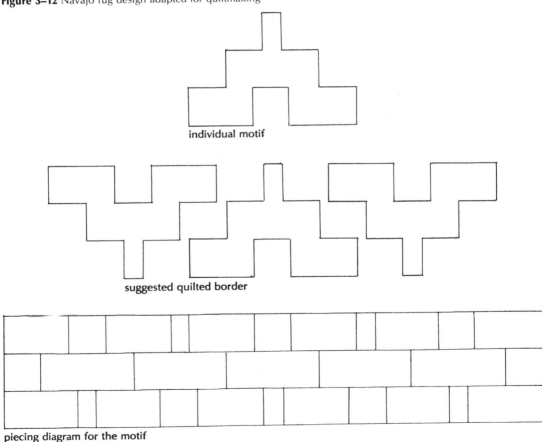

individual motif

suggested quilted border

piecing diagram for the motif

each time. When you find a variation you like, trace in the initial design so you will have a complete motif.

The last design to be given in this chapter is borrowed from a Navajo rug (Figure 3-12). It is often repeated to form a border in rugs. I have found the motif useful to frame appliqué designs, as can be seen on my blouse that appears with the Navajo skirt in the color section. The motif can also be repeated as a quilting design. This quilting pattern can be stitched with all the motifs pointed in the same direction as has been done in the appliqué border, or a different effect can be achieved by alternating the motifs, as is shown in the second row of Figure 3-12. This is another design that adapts quite readily to piecework. In this case, strip piecing would be the technique of choice. This pieced design is seen in the bottom illustration in Figure 3-12. The individual motif is not as evident in this illustration, but with close inspection, you can see that it is present. Proper color placement will allow the design to emerge as the strips are being pieced.

FOUR

INTERPRETING THE ENVIRONMENT
IN QUILT DESIGNS

Putting impressions of the environment into fabric has always been part of the quiltmaking craft. This chapter contains designs and ideas that will help you begin to develop your own interpretations of the influences around you.

Figures 4-1 and 4-2 are typical scenes from the southwestern area of the country. The first shows the landscape that is seen in the Sonoran Desert of Arizona. The Painted Desert after a light snowfall is shown in the second photograph. No patterns have been given for the subjects in these particular photographs. They are provided simply to suggest ways to study the environment.

There are several features to be aware of when you are developing designs for quilts from pictures such as these. One is color. We saw how well it can be used in the designs developed by the quiltmakers featured earlier in the book. It is relatively easy to choose the colors for these quilts: blue for sky, earth tones for mountains, green for plants, etc. What has not been studied as closely is the subtle shadings that may also be necessary to obtain the design you have conceived. It is these shadings that give life to what might otherwise be a flat picture. To be more aware of these subtle changes in color, I sometimes find it helpful to look at black-and-white pictures rather than color.

Sometimes when examining a color photograph you are so struck by the vivid colors that your eye does not focus on the delicate changes that take place from one hue to another within these colors. It is these changes that

Figure 4–1 Sonoran Desert scene. The trees are paloverde. The tall spindly plant is ocotillo

Figure 4–2 Painted Desert of northern Arizona

give definition and depth to the landscape. With a black-and-white picture, you will need to be more aware of the changes to fully appreciate what you are seeing in the pictures. This is especially evident in the photograph of the Painted Desert. Even without full color, one can appreciate the scene by being aware of the white of the snow changing to the grays and finally the blacks of the hills. Note how clearly the horizontal striations and the vertical furrows of the mounds appear in the pictures because of changes in tone. You will find you accomplish a lot in your designing by working with different shades and being as concerned with tones as with pure color.

Shape and texture are other important qualities to consider, and here again, I believe that black-and-white photographs can help you become more aware. By taking away color, we have removed the property that first draws you to a subject. This gives you the opportunity to focus more on other properties of the design that may appeal to you.

Study again Figures 4-1 and 4-2 and decide what appeals to you. Perhaps it is the channels created in the desert floor by the slowly melting snow. Maybe it is the dimpled look created in the flat pads of the prickly pear as the spines stand in clusters. Notice the trees and shrubs on the desert scene. With the thick foliage and closely growing vegetation, no tree shape or individual branches are defined, yet the picture provides a distinct impression of the foliage that is present. In black and white, we can see that some areas are darker, and that some of the plants have a coarse texture while others have a more softly brushed appearance. Rather than simply thinking green for trees, we think more about the print of a fabric that could provide us with this variegated surface texture.

As has been shown in these examples, it is a good practice to look at black-and-white as well as color photography when developing your designs for patchwork and appliqué. Photography books available at most libraries are a good reference. There are masters of black-and-white photography who have been able to capture all of the properties just discussed, and studying

Figure 4–3 Salt River Canyon, Arizona; note horseshoe and stair-step formations on canyon wall

their work would be beneficial. Ansel Adams's black-and-white photography of the Southwest is a superior example that is well worth examining. You will find that learning to work with tones rather than color alone will greatly expand your ability in quilt design.

Next, look at the photograph of a canyon in Figure 4-3. In the absence of color in this picture, the most striking property to which we are drawn is shape. Notice the horseshoe shapes of the canyon walls, and also the stair steps carved on the edge of each formation. These shapes give rise to many design possibilities. Perhaps it was seeing a view such as this that led a craftsman many years ago to conceive the design shown in Figure 4-4. This is a design that has been used on Native American pottery for many years. The motif consists of the two large quarter circles at the top. The smaller designs show how the motif appears as it is repeated to form a border design. Notice how closely elements of the design resemble shapes in the canyon, and how the two quarter circles form a horseshoe shape. The small circle within the design may be seen as representing the sun shining in the canyon.

This half-circle design has the potential for several uses in quiltmaking. Appliqué and reverse appliqué quickly come to mind. Any combination of quarter circles might be used to achieve a variety of results. As given, the half circle might be appliquéd on a border or in the triangular space created when a block is set on point. Repeat the design to create a full circle, and you have created a design suitable for appliqué on a square quilt block. A quarter circle alone might be used in a corner where two borders come together.

This motif also has many possibilities as a linear pattern to be used for the quilting design. It can be repeated as shown to create a decorative border to complement the piecework or appliqué used in the main body of the quilt. The same process of adding or deleting quarter circles as was suggested for appliqué can be used to create quilting motifs suitable for many areas. Stippling areas of the motif would provide further accent. Actually changing

Figure 4–4 Typical Native American pottery design

two quarter circles make the complete motif

suggested use of motif to make quilted border

areas of the design is also a possibility. For example, you may choose to have fewer or more stair steps, or you may decide a second line of quilting following the same path would be attractive. Again, it is a design you will need to experiment with to find the motif most appealing to you.

As is evident from the crafts we have examined, many designs derived from nature appear quite stylized in the final product. This is true of several designs I have developed which were inspired by the saguaro cactus. This sentinel of the desert can grow to fifty feet tall and have a few or many arms. Figure 4-5 shows several specimens. A distinguishing feature of the cactus is the vertical ribs extending the entire height. The spines of the cactus are clustered in groups along the outer edge of these ribs. Figure 4-6 gives a detailed view of this characteristic. It was while inspecting this ribbing closer that I conceived the designs shown in Figure 4-7.

Figure 4–5 Several specimens of saguaro cactus, which can grow to fifty feet tall

Figure 4–6 Close-up view of ribs and spines of saguaro cactus; note how the spines are clustered and also the pattern of the shadows

The designs in the figure are appropriate for use on the lattice and border areas of a quilt. The components most apparent in the detail of the saguaro are the long vertical lines and the lines created as the shadows of the spines are cast onto the surface of the cactus. These are the two characteristics present in all of the designs. Obviously, simple geometric designs such as this are far from original; many similar designs can be found.

In the first design, four vertical lines represent the ribs, and these are connected by a series of diagonal lines reminiscent of the spines. The two vertical lines in the center may represent the edge of a rib or an indentation

Figure 4–7 Quilting designs suggested by the configuration of the saguaro ribs shown in Figure 4-6

between ribs, depending on how you focus on the design. I see this middle portion representing the edge of the rib and the horizontal lines across the narrow space creating squares that might represent the clusters of spines. An alternative would be to omit the horizontal lines.

The center motif again makes use of the vertical and diagonal lines. The

Figure 4–8 Suggested border designs for quilting: the center motif is a stylized cactus; the other two borders are suggestive of mountains

Figure 4–9 Detailed view of the configuration of the juncture of the ribs at the end of the cactus arm

lines here are more widely spaced and create an arrow-like effect. Note also on this design that the halves of the design are not evenly aligned. The design might be completed like this, creating an interesting offset result, or either of the two halves might be used alone. The final motif on Figure 4-7 is a typical zigzag or streak-of-lightning design. It might also be used to represent the rib formation and the deep furrows caused by these ribs.

A very stylized cactus is shown in the center border design of Figure 4-8. This depiction of the saguaro, with an arm to each side, is common. Saguaros such as this are frequently woven into Tohono O'odham baskets. This is a

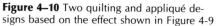

Figure 4–10 Two quilting and appliqué designs based on the effect shown in Figure 4-9

simple design to draft on graph paper as it is simply a block design. Length and width can be changed to fit any border by simply extending the cactus across more blocks when drafting the pattern. This is also a versatile design because there is no wrong way. Every other saguaro is rotated so there is not an up and down to the pattern.

We will continue with the saguaro as a design source for the next several patterns. Figure 4-9 gives a detailed view of the configuration of the juncture of the ribs at the end of the arm. The two designs in Figure 4-10 repeat this twisting effect. Again, these motifs are suitable for appliqué or quilting, and the designs can be expanded. The motif of the lower design could be worked in a combination of piecing and appliqué. The sections of the design would be pieced and then the unit as a whole appliquéd to the background in the same fashion as the "Dresden Plate" design.

Another design taken from the saguaro is much more realistic. The photograph in Figure 4-11 shows a typical saguaro arm formation. The arms here are seen beginning at about the same level on the body, although this is not always the case. The two arms at the sides create the typical shape people associate with the cactus. This simple shape can be used to create a plain, yet effective quilting design. A close view of the motif in stitching can be seen in Figure 4-12. An illustration of the motif is given in Figure 4-13.

The final design given for the saguaro is simply an addition to a traditional design. To the "Moon over the Mountain" design, a single saguaro has been added. This gives the block a western flair and yet maintains the simple lines of the original design. A sample of this block can be seen in Figure 4-14. Figure 4-15 is an illustration of the complete design. Figure 4-16 is a full-size pattern of the cactus to appliqué on a standard 12" block. Please note that the body of the cactus is given in two pieces. To make the length necessary for the block, $5\frac{1}{2}$" should be added between the dotted lines. In addition, notice that the arms of the cactus are in different positions on Figures 4-14 and 4-15. This is to demonstrate that there are several design possibilities; the saguaro arms should be placed in any position that is pleasing to you.

The animals of the Southwest are another important design source from the environment, and as evidenced by several of the quilts that have been shown, they are a popular subject. Coyotes are especially popular at present. They are found as figurines, in jewelry, and on clothing, among other things. As a result of this popularity, I thought it appropriate to design a coyote

Figure 4–11 Typical saguaro arm formation that makes a simple appliqué or quilting design

Figure 4–12 Detailed view of saguaro quilting motif

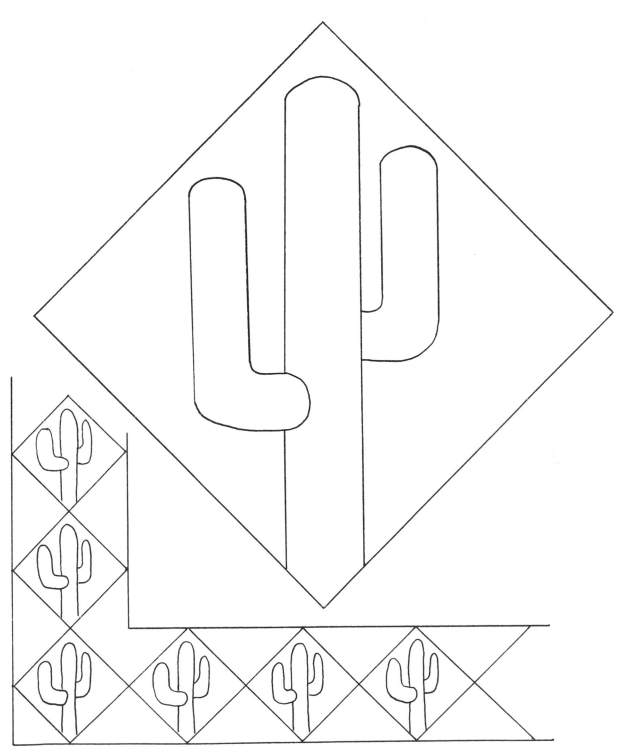

Figure 4–13 Saguaro quilting motif and suggested use for border design

Figure 4–14 Example of appliquéd "Moon over the Mountain" design with saguaro

Figure 4–15 "Moon over the Mountain" with saguaro

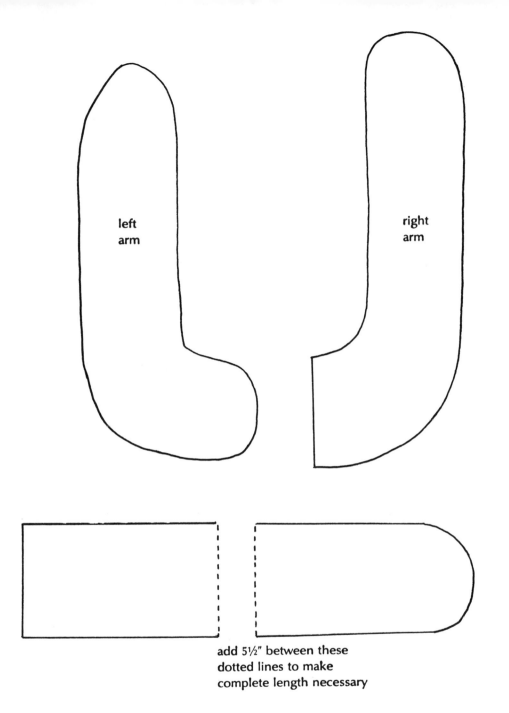

left
arm

right
arm

**add 5½" between these
dotted lines to make
complete length necessary**

add seam allowances to all pieces

Figure 4–16 Full-size pattern for saguaro cactus to be used on a standard 12" "Moon over the Mountain" block

Figure 4–17 Detail of appliqué and quilting on blouse

Figure 4–18 Detail of appliqué and quilting around coyote block; note stair-step motif, which is common in southwestern weaving

Figure 4–19 Close-up of appliquéd coyote design

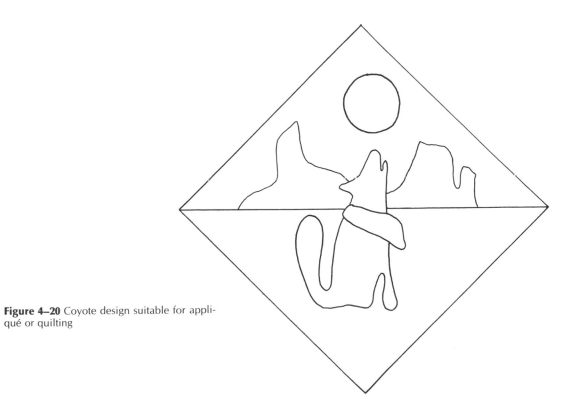

Figure 4–20 Coyote design suitable for appliqué or quilting

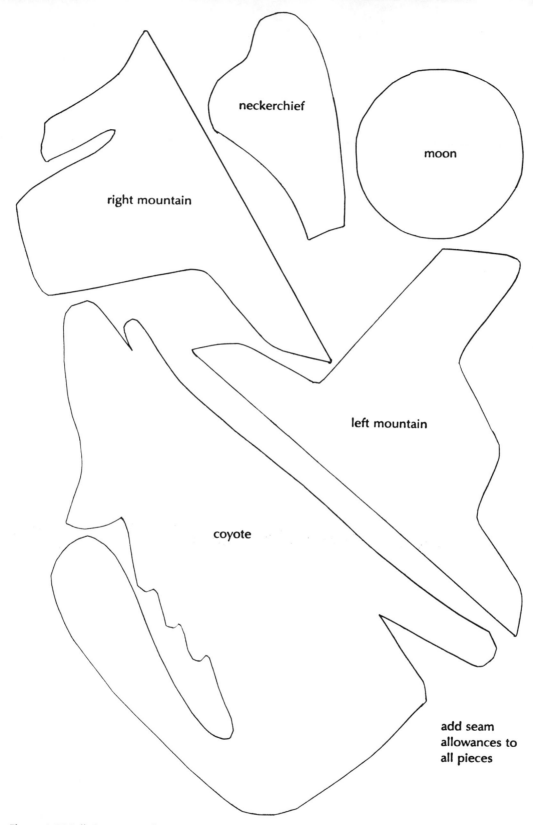

right mountain

neckerchief

moon

left mountain

coyote

add seam
allowances to
all pieces

Figure 4–21 Full-size patterns for coyote block

square for this book. The square can be seen on the blouse in the color section of this book. The skirt shown is a traditional Navajo broomstick skirt. It is three-tiered and has fine pleats throughout each tier. The name was derived because the skirt is wrapped on a broomstick to maintain the pleats.

After obtaining the skirt described, I wanted to design an appropriate quilted garment to wear with it, and as I was also designing for this book, the design for the coyote and the blouse came about. Although not visible in the picture, the pleats of the skirt have been repeated horizontally for a front panel of the blouse and vertically on the sleeves (the coyote block is on the blouse back). The side fronts of the blouse continue the floral design in appliqué and quilting that was begun on the back of the blouse. This floral design was obtained by copying the print of the skirt. The entire blouse outside of the block is quilted every $\frac{1}{4}$", again to repeat the lines of the pleating of the skirt. Figures 4-17 and 4-18 show detail of the appliqué and the quilting designs.

The coyote is designed to fit on a $7\frac{1}{2}$ to 8" block. Set on point, the top half of the block should be one color and the bottom half a different color. In the block shown, tan was used for the top and salmon for the bottom. The mountain formations are deep maroon, the moon white, and the coyote gray. A green neckerchief has been added to the coyote for accent. The block can be further adorned with embroidery. Figure 4-19 is a close-up of the block, and Figure 4-20 provides the design. Full-size patterns for this design have been provided in Figure 4-21. Remember to add a seam allowance to each pattern piece.

Figure 5–1 Simplified pueblo design appliquéd on a single block

FIVE

SOUTHWESTERN ARCHITECTURE AS A DESIGN SOURCE

The architecture of the Southwest seems to have been designed with the quilt artist in mind. Graceful curves and plentiful geometric designs abound. The styles used are rich in detail work, providing an ample source of ideas. The doors, windows, beams, and other components can all be used to develop motifs for appliqué, quilting, and piecework. Developing these ideas follows in the longstanding tradition of quiltmakers being inspired by the dwellings of an area. Who is not familiar with the log cabin barn-raising pattern, attic windows, castle wall, church steps, schoolhouse, or hole-in-the-barn-door designs? As is the custom, the designs may be either realistic or stylized and based on a complete subject or just an element of a building.

One of the earliest architectural styles of the region is that of the Pueblo Indians. Their adobe pueblos are often multi-storied structures. Some, such as the well known Acoma, or Sky City, of northern New Mexico, sit atop mesas. The structures are flat-roofed and resemble rectangles stacked one on the other in a random fashion. Distinguishing features include wood-framed windows and doors, vigas (wooden beams), and wooden ladders leading from one level to the next. This simple design has been used by many quilters who wanted to capture a typical scene of the area in their quilts.

Figure 5-1 shows a simplified version of the pueblo design that is suitable for an individual appliquéd quilt block. In this motif, a single pueblo home has been separated from what would be a grouping of houses and is depicted standing alone in the desert. A diagram for the design is given in Figure 5-2. This is only one of several ways in which the pueblo design could be used on a block. For instance, the cactus might be omitted, or smaller plants might be embroidered around the home. In another version, a row of mountains might be put behind the pueblo to give a feeling of depth to the scene. Further details might also be added through embroidery and appliqué, such as pottery sitting in front of the home.

A full-size pattern, sized for a standard 12″ block, has been given in Figure 5-3. Allowance for turning under should be added to each piece. The saguaro is made from the same pattern as was used for the "Moon over the Mountain" block (Figure 4-16). The sun should be made from a $2\frac{1}{4}$″ circle (before seam allowance is added). All other pieces necessary to construct the pueblo are given in the figure.

Figure 5–2 Diagram of pueblo design suitable for appliqué or quilting

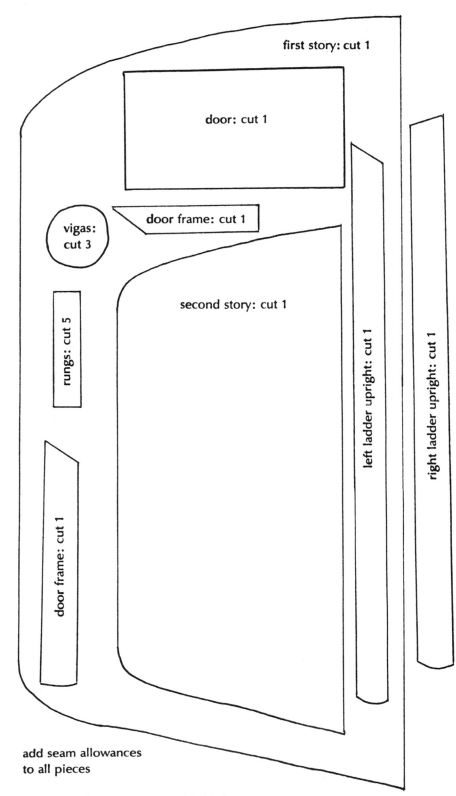

first story: cut 1

door: cut 1

door frame: cut 1

vigas:
cut 3

second story: cut 1

rungs: cut 5

left ladder upright: cut 1

right ladder upright: cut 1

door frame: cut 1

add seam allowances
to all pieces

Figure 5–3 Full-size pattern for pueblo block

The design of the pueblo block is also suitable as a quilting pattern. When I do the block in quilting, I usually add rays to the sun and stitch ribs into the cactus. The design can also be adapted in a number of ways for quilting. For example, the pueblo can be centered in a block and a cross-hatching design stitched in the background, or stippling can be added to emphasize doors, windows, etc.

Reminiscent of this pueblo style is the modern adobe construction covered with stucco, which is a common sight in the region. The lines are usually very simple and favor rounded edges and corners. Vigas are seen

Figure 5–4 Typical Santa Fe style architecture

protruding from the exteriors of the buildings, and window ledges and door frames are often thick wooden pieces that echo the beams. Figure 5-4 shows an example of this style. White, tan, or a sandy pink color are the most common tints seen in the exterior walls. This type of building has come to represent the area for many people and can be seen in some contemporary quilts. The photograph may be considered a starting point for ideas for quilt designs. In addition to seeing it simply as a building that can be easily

Figure 5–5 San Xavier del Bac Mission, front facade

rendered in appliqué, look at it for the angles and shapes and how these might be used to develop patchwork and quilting designs.

Don't neglect to look at the shadows cast by the trees onto the building. Is there a design apparent? Also look at what can be done to reproduce this shadowing effect if you choose to appliqué the building and trees. Perhaps there is a piece of fabric that would give the impression of this design, or maybe you would want to dye or paint fabric to achieve the desired effect.

From the relative simplicity of design of the pueblo and "Santa Fe" styles, we will now look at the other end of the spectrum, where some of the same components are maintained, but the building style is much more ornate. The Southwest has numerous missions as a result of Spanish colonization of the area, and these provide excellent subject matter for the fiber artist.

Perhaps the most beautiful of all missions of the Southwest, San Xavier del Bac, stands just outside of Tucson. It is a heavily ornamented structure, completed in the late 1700s. Figure 5-5 shows the building's front facade. Note the extensive use of arches, both in entryways and on the towers. Scrolls can be seen in the upper part of the facade and on the arches to the sides of the towers. As we have seen, scrolls and arches are found in many quilt designs. Also notice the stair-step configuration at the top of the gate. This, too, is a popular design in southwestern art. These are the obvious designs that are first apparent, but there are numerous design possibilities to be found by studying this mission and other buildings like it.

One possible design to consider is a border motif drawn from elements of the railing at the bottom of the towers. These octagonal towers, with short sides alternating with longer sides, are also a good design source. Again, as has been suggested with the other pictures, study this one and take elements from it that you find interesting to develop your own designs.

Figure 5-6 shows the same building from another angle, which presents different design opportunities. As is clearly visible in both pictures, this edifice is an excellent subject for the appliqué artist. Some of the details might be

Figure 5–6 San Xavier del Bac Mission, side view

a test of skill, but it would be a workable project. This might be done as a simple rendition of the mission on a single block, or there is sufficient background and foreground subject matter to create a full fabric painting.

Another possibility is to make a line drawing of a building such as this in a very stylized form, using mainly straight lines and eliminating curves and ornate details. Although this would not produce an exact reproduction, it could be an interesting pattern. Such a design could be done in patchwork instead of appliqué.

Because of their unique architectural style, missions are a popular motif in art from the area. However, not all are as ornate or complex as San Xavier. Figure 5-7 shows what remains of the Tumacacori Mission in southern Ari-

Figure 5–7 Tumacacori Mission

zona. Because the style of this mission is much less ornate, this subject would be less complicated to execute in fiber.

Figure 5-8 shows a work in progress that suggests a simplified design. It is not an accurate rendition of any one mission, but instead is a composite of several design elements. The mission was created by simply stacking rectangle upon rectangle, with an arch added to the upper two sections. This arch was repeated in the window and door, as well as being used to frame the piece. This idea originated after I saw the mission in Figure 5-7.

Figure 5–8 ''Mission View,'' © 1985 by Mary Evangeline Dillon. This is an adaptation of the design, being completed as a wall quilt

The next design started as a quilting motif designed to fill in blocks on a western-design quilt (Figure 5-9). The initial design consisted solely of the mission shape. Deciding this did not adequately fill the block, I added the sun and then the hills. Finally, the rays leading into the mission were added to balance with the lines in the upper portion of the block.

This design can be rendered in appliqué or in a combination of piecework and appliqué. To make a combination block, I pieced all of the background. This included the rays around the sun and the hills. The only appliquéd pieces were the mission and a circle of fabric for the sun. An alternative might involve piecing only two pieces of fabric for the background—one suitable for the sky and one for the ground. The hills, mission, and sun would

Figure 5–9 Mission motif suitable for quilting, appliqué, or a combination of piecing and appliqué

Figure 5–10 Typical recessed area in southwestern-style architecture. Note the tile with the religious scene

then be appliquéd. The effect of the rays would be eliminated, but this element could be added again to the design during the quilting process.

As has been apparent in much we have already looked at, arches and curves tend to dominate many architectural styles of the Southwest. In the final part of this chapter, we will look at how these individual elements can be a source of quilting designs.

Small recesses or nooks in the walls, both exterior and interior, are common in southwestern architecture. These recessed shelves commonly have been used to hold religious figures, but other artwork is also displayed. Figure 5-10 is an example of one of these recessed areas. This is a simple design, but these areas can be much more ornate.

The upper portion of one of these more ornate recesses is shown in Figure 5-11. It presents a clamshell-type design, a motif not unfamiliar to quilt-makers. This design is easily transposed into a quilting motif. One suggestion for design is shown in Figure 5-12. The motif is especially suitable for a triangular, plain area of a quilt. This triangular area occurs when blocks are set on point or in an eight-pointed star pattern. Note on the illustration that

Figure 5–11 Ornate design found on top of nook in wall. Note that it forms a clamshell

Figure 5–12 Quilting motif based on clam-shell design in Figure 5-11

the size of the motif can be adjusted to fit different size triangles within the same piece of work. This is another design that can be repeated for a border motif. This could be done with the curve of the motifs always pointed in one direction, or it can be flip-flopped to form an alternating design. Also, two motifs might be used together to form a complete circle for a square block.

The next quilt designs were inspired by a design element that is quite common to the area. The design can be seen in the opening in the wall shown in Figure 5-13 and again following along the top of the wall in Figure 5-14. I do not know whether there is a name for this shape, but I describe

Figure 5–13 Typical opening found in walls of the Southwest

Figure 5–14 The arch shown on this gate is typical of southwestern architecture

it as an oval with corners. It is a pleasing design that is adaptable enough to fit many areas.

A number of variations on this motif are possible. Two are presented in Figure 5-15. The first variation simply presents the design with three rows of stitching. The potential to add to this is obvious. This type of design tends to form a picture-frame effect. Thus the open central space can be filled with a separate quilting or appliqué motif. The design can also be repeated over and over to fill a block, thus creating an echoing effect.

In the second part of the figure, two sides have been elongated and straightened, thus creating a rectangular motif. A simple diamond motif has been added to the center of the rectangle, creating a much different effect.

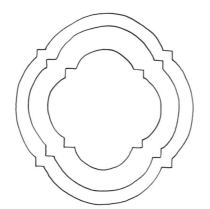

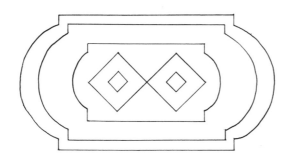

Figure 5–15 Two quilting motifs based on typical arches and wall openings

This is an excellent design for rectangular blocks or as a repetitive design for a border. Obviously, this motif also has the potential for many variations. Replacing the center diamonds with another motif and adding more lines of echoing to the outer portion of the motif are only two possibilities that come to mind. As has been suggested earlier, you may want to use tracing paper to experiment with adding or subtracting elements of the designs.

Further quilting designs are shown in the border motifs in Figure 5-16. Although not exact renditions of any one architectural design element, all

Figure 5–16 Border quilting designs

Figure 5–17 Typical wooden gates found in the region

Figure 5–18 Carved wooden balcony

of these borders were inspired by some line or form in southwestern architecture. Figures 5-17, 5-18, and 5-19 show some of these elements.

The top border in Figure 5-16 was inspired by the diagonal cross bars on a gate similar to that pictured in Figure 5-17. Note that squares or diamonds might be used to fill in areas of the design. It is also possible to adjust the angle at which the cross patterns meet. An increase or decrease in this angle will further elongate the patterns or square the patterns.

The middle border uses elements found on the balcony pictured in Figure 5-18. Note the carved circles in the upright supports. Splitting these in half, I used one half from each of two uprights, positioning these sections back to back. This created the motif as shown with the curved diamond in between the circles. I then added the smaller diamond to complete the space and add a point of interest. The bottom border draws elements from many common designs.

Figure 5-20 shows another quilting design that reflects the southwestern

Figure 5–19 Typical balcony of the region

Figure 5–20 Quilting motif reflecting architectural details

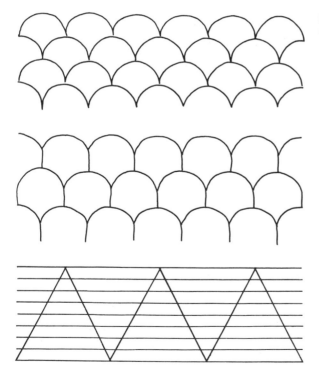

Figure 5–21 Fill-in or background quilting motifs

style of architecture. This close-up view comes from Miles Merkel's *High Desert* quilt.

Figure 5-21 gives three ideas for background or fill-in designs based on the other motifs we have looked at. The first is the clamshell design, again well known to quiltmakers. This design is common in art forms from many regions including the Southwest and can be used with some southwestern designs. The middle design is a variation of the first clamshell design. It is common to see this motif on pottery. Note that the design has been elongated to be more representative of arches. The bottom design would be suitable for a border or sashing.

SIX

CONSTRUCTING QUILTING DESIGNS

In the preceding chapters of the book, I have taken examples from art, architecture, and nature to show you how you can transfer a concept developed from observations of these things into a usable pattern for quiltmaking. In this final chapter I will review a few more designs with you and in the process explain how they were developed and drafted.

Many of the designs we have examined are from pottery and basketry and therefore have been circular. These designs might appear more difficult to draft at first, but for the most part they can be drafted easily with the right tools.

If available, a circular type of graph paper is useful. It is available with the engineering forms at many office supply stores and some art stores. It has many concentric circles and also has the degrees of the circles marked so that you can easily divide the area into eight, twelve, or whatever number of divisions is required. I try to make use of this graph paper whenever possible as it is a real time saver.

In the absence of paper such as this, you can make your own substitute. Start by drawing a series of concentric circles with a compass. How many you draw and the spacing of the circles will depend on the type of design you plan to do. I usually draw more circles than I will need, and I vary the distance between these circles. Drawing extra circles at the beginning, even if these are not used later, is much easier than adding circles later.

After drawing the circles, I use a protractor to divide them into the necessary parts. This is easily accomplished with some simple division. Knowing a circle has 360 degrees, you need only divide this number by the number of sections you want to divide the circle into, and this will give you the degrees or reading you will need to mark. For example, 360 divided by 4 is 90, so the circle must be marked every 90 degrees to divide it into fourths. A circle divided into twelve parts would need to be marked every 30 degrees, etc. To make the marks, I first draw a line directly through the center of the circle. Then, laying the protractor on this line, exactly centered, I do all of

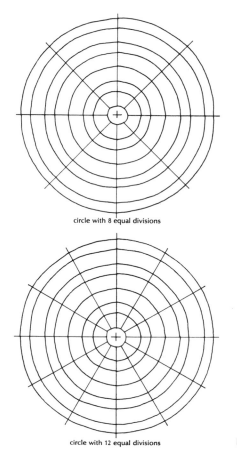

circle with 8 equal divisions

circle with 12 equal divisions

Figure 6–1 Circular graphs

the markings for half the circle. I then repeat this procedure for the other half. These marks are connected with a line to the center of the circle or the opposite mark to complete the process. In the case of odd-numbered divisions, one section will straddle the line that marks the halfway point of the circle. For example, a circle divided for the five-pointed star motif will have $2\frac{1}{2}$ sections in each half circle. Two diagrams that have been made in this manner are shown in Figure 6-1. The top figure has eight divisions, the lower figure has twelve.

The motifs shown in Figure 6-2 are variations on some of the common baskets we examined earlier. The top design is in six parts, so I divided my

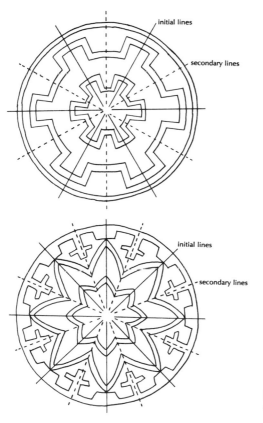

Figure 6–2 Typical basket designs drafted for quilt patterns

circle into six sections using the protractor and marking a line every 60 degrees. As can be seen, these initial markings go through the center of each section of the motif. I next marked secondary lines to center the indented parts of the motif. With the design placed over a circular graph like that in Figure 6-1, I marked the remaining designs using the concentric circles as guides.

This same process can be used for the bottom figure, but eight initial divisions are necessary. This provides the points of both the large and small star patterns. Eight secondary divisions need to be drawn to create the point where the indentation falls between the points of the stars. The crosses of the outer border will fall on these same lines. Degrees to each side of this second set of lines would be measured to determine the width of the arms of the cross and of the notched design of the outer border. Sets of concentric circles would be necessary to complete the design.

As you can see, this can be a time-consuming, but not impossible process. This is why the circular graph paper is so useful. All of the circles and lines have already been marked, so the step of drawing all of these, and of mea-suring degrees, etc., is eliminated. If you are doing numerous sketches, it is worthwhile to use this paper and eliminate some steps.

Most of the graph paper such as this is not large enough to do a full-size motif for a large square, so it will still be necessary to draft your own circles and divisions for the design you choose to make. However, it is much easier to do this only once than to repeat the process for every sketch you may be trying en route to this final design. If you will be drafting several large motifs, you can save time by drawing one large set of circles with all the divisions, then using tracing paper over this to complete further designs. This way you need not draw your graph repeatedly.

Using this process you can produce the symmetry found in the circular designs of baskets and pottery. I suggest you practice with the compass and protractor for a while to perfect the technique. You can also copy the graphs of Figure 6-1 and use them to begin developing your own designs.

A circular graph has also been used to produce the "Father Sun" design shown in Figure 6-3. Note the concentric circles in the center. To the circles, twelve initial divisions were added at 30-degree intervals to give the twelve points of the sun at the tip of the triangles. Twelve secondary divisions were then made midway between the initial divisions. The points at which the secondary lines crossed the outer concentric circles served as guides from which to draw the sides of the triangles.

The upper half of the motif was left with just the design created from these initial steps. To the bottom half, lines were added within the triangles to add to the interest of the design. If the design is quilted, the solid small triangles shown in solid black might be created through stippling. In an

Figure 6–3 "Father Sun" design

appliquéd design, these would simply be stitched on, or embroidery would be a possibility.

The process of developing a typical zigzag design is illustrated in Figure 6-4. This is an extremely simple design to draw using a standard square graph as illustrated in the top drawing. Squares are simply divided diagonally to produce the desired effect. The middle drawing illustrates how the design would appear if the unnecessary graph lines were removed. This also shows you the minimum divisions that would be necessary to piece a design such as this. As you can see, diamonds and triangles would be the piecing units. The design might also be pieced using the divisions in the first illustration. This would consist entirely of triangles and would give a tile-like appearance to the work. In the bottom illustration all the extra lines have been removed, leaving just the zigzag or streak-of-lightning design. In this form, the motif is suitable for quilting.

A design such as that illustrated in Figure 6-5 has been shown earlier in the text. To draft a design such as this, start with graph paper. The design consists simply of vertical lines with diagonal lines drawn across squares in

Figure 6–4 Steps in drafting typical zigzag design

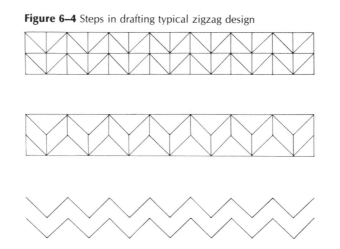

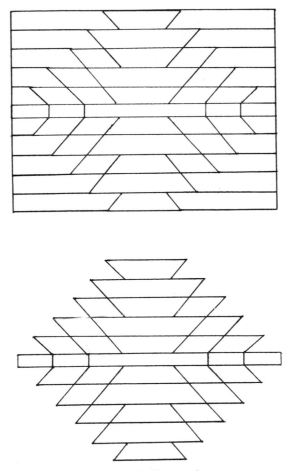

Figure 6–5 Typical design built using the stair-step method

somewhat the same method as was used in the zigzag pattern. The horizontal lines of the graph have been left in the top drawing of the figure to show how the divisions are achieved. The vertical lines have been omitted to make it easier to see the motif. The bottom drawing shows how the final design would appear.

All of the designs in Figure 6-6 are built from the same starting unit. This simple stair-step design can be drawn easily on graph paper; and you need only count squares to achieve the desired look. For the top line, for example, you would start at the left side, draw across three squares, up one, over one, up one, over two, up one, over one, and then repeat the process in reverse to go down the other side. This is repeated as often as necessary to obtain the length of line necessary. A second line has been added by stepping up one square on the graph. The first line is echoed, always maintaining this one-square separation. Third and fourth lines can be added in the same way.

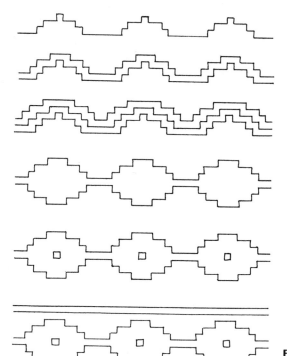

Figure 6–6 Border quilting motifs that were created starting with the first line of stair steps and building from there

The three designs comprising the bottom half of Figure 6-6 represent the steps used to build a final design. Or any of these three designs could be used alone. All were completed by simply counting squares on the graph paper. This versatile design can be elongated, shortened, or made to appear more diamond-shaped, depending on the type of motif you desire, how intricately you want the quilting to be done, and the space to be filled.

I drafted the top motif in Figure 6-7 by counting squares as for the stair-step design in Figure 6-6. Elements can be easily added to or deleted from this design, again depending on the size and intricacy you wish for your quilting design.

I drafted the lower figure using standard square graph paper. As was done for the zigzag motif in Figure 6-4, I obtained all of the lines for this

Figure 6–7 Quilting motifs suitable for oblong spaces

design by using the diagonal lines of the squares. This motif is good for filling in an oblong space. As is, it is rather intricate. You can simplify the design by deleting elements. One suggestion would be to maintain only the two small squares and the large cross formation in the central part of the motif, while deleting the two zigzag lines to each side.

The final few designs shown are a series of border motifs all based on arrows. Note the design in the wooden door shown in Figure 6-8. Designs

Figure 6–8 Wooden door of adobe house

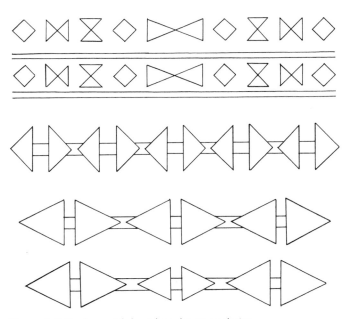

Figure 6–9 Border motifs based on the arrow design

such as this are seen frequently in the Southwest. Using this for inspiration, I developed the borders in Figure 6-9. Again, all of these designs were drawn by simply counting squares on graph paper and connecting these through a series of horizontal, vertical, and diagonal lines. The first two designs are the same, but two lines of quilting have been added to each side of the second row to create a more finished effect.

The last three triangular designs are the same, but sizes and angles of the triangles have been altered to achieve different looks. Changing the length and angle of the triangles is easy to accomplish on graph paper. For the triangle shown in the third row, count out from this point the same number of squares in two directions. Then draw a diagonal line between these two points. For example, count two squares over and two squares up and draw a diagonal line. You can see this gives you half of a square. To achieve the more elongated triangles seen in the last two borders of the page, you will need a diagonal of a rectangle instead of a square. For example, you might choose to count three squares up from a point on a line and mark a second point. To achieve the longer triangles, count four or five squares over from the first point, and draw a diagonal line between the second and third points. You can see that what has been created is the diagonal half of a rectangle. This gives you half of your final triangular shape.

Now that you have seen how southwestern designs can be achieved in your quiltmaking, I hope that you will use the techniques you have learned in the book to create your own designs for quilts. The techniques may be used to design quilts from any region. The other quiltmakers and I all enjoy the sharing that is found in the quiltmaking world. I hope that by sharing our quilts and ideas in the book, new areas of the quiltmaking process will now be available to you.

LIST OF QUILTMAKERS

Addresses for the quiltmakers who welcome inquiries are given below. If the quiltmaker teaches or sells patterns or quilts, this information is noted.

Ellen Anderson
4418 S. Rita Lane
Tempe, AZ 85282

Marva Dalebout
1175 E. 900 So., #6
St. George, UT 84770
(lectures and workshops)

Mary Evangeline Dillon
"Blooms of the Desert Designs"
6149 E. Broadway
Box 225
Tucson, AZ 85711
(patterns, books, lectures, and workshops)

Gail Garber
820 Western Hills Dr.
Rio Rancho, NM 87124
(patterns, lectures, and workshops)

Martha Leeds
P.O. Box 271
New Laguna, NM 87038
(quilts and other artwork)

Stan Lucero
P.O. Box 1406
Pueblo of Laguna, NM 87026
(quilts and clothing, other artwork)

Roxanne McElroy
"Designs by Roxanne"
57 West Eden Elm Circle
The Woodlands, TX 77381
(patterns, lectures, and workshops)

Miles Merkel
2240 Golf Links Rd.
Sierra Vista, AZ 85635
(patterns, book)

Isabel Merrell
136 N. 9th E.
Brigham City, UT 84302

Connee Sager
4561 Caminito Callado
Tucson, AZ 85718

Teri Stewart
17643 Ave. 288
Exeter, CA 93221

Pauline Trout
"Quail and Poppy Designs"
1189 W. Evergreen
Rialto, CA 92376
(patterns)

BIBLIOGRAPHY

Bahti, Mark. *Pueblo Stories and Storytellers*. Tucson: Treasure Chest Publications, 1988.

Bahti, Tom. *Southwestern Indian Ceremonials*. Las Vegas: KC Publications, 1970.

Brackman, Barbara. *An Encyclopedia of Pieced Quilt Patterns,* vols. 1–8. Lawrence, Kans.: Prairie Flower Publications, 1979–83.

Callander, Lee A., and Fawcett, David M. *Native American Painting*. New York: Museum of the American Indian, 1982.

DeWald, Terry. *The Papago Indians and Their Basketry*. Tucson: Terry DeWald, 1979.

Fontana, Bernard L., et al. *Papago Indian Pottery*. Seattle: University of Washington Press, 1962.

Harlow, Francis H., and Young, John V. *Contemporary Pueblo Indian Pottery*. Santa Fe: Museum of New Mexico Press, 1965.

Kennedy, Paul E. *North American Indian Design Coloring Book*. New York: Dover Publications, 1971.

Khin, Yvonne M. *The Collector's Dictionary of Quilt Names and Patterns*. Washington, D.C.: Acropolis Books, 1980.

Mauldin, Barbara. *Traditions in Transition*. Santa Fe: Museum of New Mexico Press, 1984.

INDEX

Missions
  Mesilla, 84
  San Xavier del Bac, 147–149
  Tumacacori, 149–150
"Moon over the Mountain" quilt block, 133, 136
"Moon over the Mountain with Saguaro" quilt block, 133, 136, 137

"Navajo" quilt block, 6
Navajo Rug Makers quilt (Dalebout), 99, color section
"New Mexico Star" quilt block, 6

Open weave baskets. *See* baskets

Painted Desert, 122, 123
Papago Basket quilt (Arthur), 32, 35, 36, color section
Paper-cutting method of design, 16–17
Patterns
  adaptation of traditional
    "Sun over the Mountain," 25–27
    "Moon over the Mountain with Saguaro," 133, 136, 137
  contemporary
    "Church of San Albino," 84
    "Columbia," 84
    "Cotton Bolls," 84
    "Covered Wagon," 60, 84
    "Coyote," 133, 139, 140, 141
    "Jackrabbit," 58
    "Moon over the Mountain

with Saguaro," 133, 136, 137
    pottery design, 85
    "Pueblo," 142–144
    "Roadrunner," 74, 85, 86
    "Spanish Dancers," 85, 86
    stylized saddle, 59
    thunderbird, 54, 84
    windmill, 59
  naming, 3
  redesigning, 14–17, 136
  repetition of. *See* single pattern repetition
  star, 4–6, 32, 33, 42, 45, 46, 106, 107, 110
  traditional
    "Arizona," 3, 4, 8–10, 19, 20
    "Arizona's Cactus Flower," 4, 8, 9, 10
    "Arrow," 4
    "Arrow Crown," 5
    "Arrow Points," 5, 9, 10
    "Arrowhead," 4, 5, 6
    "Arrowheads," 5, 6
    "Blossoming Cactus," 7, 11, 12
    "Cactus Basket," 3, 7, 17, 20, 24, 25, 27
    "Cactus Flower," 4
    "Broken Arrow," 6
    "Buffalo Ridge," 7, 9, 10
    "Broad Arrow," 14–15
    "Chisholm Trail," 20
    "Colorado," 7
    "Colorado Arrow," 4
    "Delectable Mountains," 80, 81
    "Desert Rose," 7
    "Devil's Claw," 6
    "Dolly Madison's Star." *See* "Santa Fe"
    "Far West," 4

    "Flower Basket." *See* "Rainbow Cactus"
    "Flying Geese," 76
    "Indian Hammer," 4, 18
    "Indian Hatchet," 5, 18
    "Indian Mats," 6
    "Indian Meadow," 6, 20, 21
    "Indian Plumes," 5
    "Indian Star," 5, 11, 12, 18
    "Indian Trail," 7
    "Jersey Tulip," *See* "Rainbow Cactus"
    "Lone Star," 5
    "Mexican Block," 6
    "Mexican Star," 4
    "Moon over the Mountain," 133, 136
    "Navajo," 6
    "New Mexican Star," 6
    "Phoenix," 4, 13
    "Prickly Pear," 3, 7, 20, 22
    "Quail's Nest," 4, 18
    "Rainbow Cactus," 7, 11, 12
    "Rocky Mountain Puzzle," 5
    "Roman Stripes," 71
    "Sage Bud," 4, 14–16
    "Santa Fe," 6
    "Santa Fe Trail," 6
    "Star of the West," 4, 12, 13
    "Tangled Arrows," 4
    "Texas Cactus Basket," 7, 11, 12
    "Texas Rose," 7
    "Texas Star," 5
    "Utah," 7
    "Wagon Tracks," 4, 18
    "Winged Arrow," 16, 17